God is Everything

Richard Lowe

The Writing King

God is Everything

Copyright © 2026 by Richard G Lowe

Disclaimer

This book is not therapy, medical treatment, or professional counseling. If you have serious mental health issues, go see a professional. If you're suicidal, call a crisis hotline. If you're in an abusive relationship, call the police or a domestic violence hotline. Don't expect a book to solve problems that require immediate professional intervention.

The ideas here come from personal experience and research, not professional credentials in psychology or counseling. Take what's useful, ignore what isn't, and don't blame me for your choices. I'm sharing perspectives, not giving you orders about how to live.

The relationship advice is based on general principles, not your specific situation. If your relationship problems are complicated or dangerous, get professional help instead of relying on books for guidance.

If you recognize yourself in the descriptions of toxic people or destructive groups, good. That awareness is the first step toward change. But don't expect this book to fix everything that's wrong in your life. Real change requires real work that goes beyond reading.

Table of Contents

See books by Richard Lowe at

https://masterofworlds.com

Get free publishing insights and industry updates at

https://thewritingking.substack.com

For ghostwriting and book coaching services see

https://thewritingking.com

Introduction

You think you know what God is. You don't.

For thousands of years, humans have imagined God as a being somewhere else. A powerful entity watching from heaven. A cosmic parent judging our choices. A voice speaking from burning bushes. Every one of these concepts misses the mark completely.

God is not a being. God is not separate from you. God is not watching you from some distant realm.

God is everything.

God is the universe itself. Every star, every planet, every particle of matter and wave of energy. God is space and time and dimension. God is life and consciousness and choice. God is the rock under your feet and the air in your lungs and the thoughts in your mind.

You are not separate from God. You are part of God. You are God experiencing itself from your unique perspective.

This isn't metaphor. This isn't poetry. This isn't a belief system to adopt on faith. It's a description of what everything actually is — including you.

Most people relate to God as an external being — powerful, distant, and fundamentally separate from human existence. God is up there, you are down here, and the relationship involves worship, obedience, and hope for divine intervention.

That entire framework is based on a misunderstanding of what God is. The separation between divine and human is an illusion that prevents you from recognizing your own true nature.

The implications extend far beyond religious belief. If you are literally God experiencing individual existence, then every aspect of human life takes on new meaning and purpose. Death becomes transition instead of ending. Relationships become encounters between different expressions of the same consciousness. Suffering becomes God exploring the full range of possible experience instead of punishment or random misfortune.

This book began as a brief exploration of these ideas. It quickly became clear that redefining God requires examining everything else: how consciousness works, what happens when you die, how to live ethically when you understand what you are, how to raise children who are also divine beings, and how to make sense of challenging aspects of existence like mental illness, evil, and meaningless suffering.

I'm not asking you to believe any of this on faith. Consider what's here and see if it makes better sense of your own experience than the alternatives you've been offered. The framework either works or it doesn't. That's the only test that matters.

This book presents ideas that will piss off a lot of people. If you're looking for feel-good spirituality that confirms what you already believe, this isn't for you. You don't have to agree with anything here. You're free to disagree, criticize, or completely reject every idea presented. That's what adults do with information — they evaluate it and make their own decisions.

Once you understand what God really is, you'll never see yourself or anything else the same way again.

God Is Not What You Think

Stop. Right now, picture God in your mind.

What did you see? A bearded man on a throne? A glowing figure in white robes? A voice without form? Maybe you went abstract and imagined pure light or infinite space.

Whatever you pictured, you're wrong.

Not partially wrong. Not close but missing some details. Completely, fundamentally wrong.

This isn't your fault. You've been taught to think of God as a "who" instead of a "what." As a being instead of being itself. As separate instead of everything.

Every religion gets this wrong. Every philosophy misses the mark. Every spiritual teacher who talks about "connecting with God" or "finding God" or "serving God" starts from a false premise.

You can't connect with God because you already are God. You can't find God because God is what you are. You can't serve God because there's no separate entity to serve.

God is not he. God is not she. God is not it. God is not a being at all.

God is existence itself.

God is the universe. Not ruling it from somewhere else. Not watching it unfold. Not occasionally intervening in its affairs. God IS the universe. Every atom, every force, every dimension, every moment of time.

When you look at a tree, you're looking at God. When you feel the wind, you're feeling God. When you think a thought, God is thinking through you. When your heart beats, that's God's heartbeat.

You are not a creation of God. You are not made in God's image. You are not God's child or servant or beloved.

You are God.

Part of God, anyway. A unique perspective through which God experiences itself. One facet of an infinite consciousness exploring every possible point of view.

This isn't metaphor. This isn't poetry. This is the literal truth about what you are and what everything is.

Most people can't handle this truth. They want God to be separate, to be other, to be someone they can pray to and blame and bargain with. They want a cosmic parent figure who will make everything okay if they just believe hard enough or follow the right rules.

But that God doesn't exist. Never did. The God you are is so much more than anything humans have imagined.

How Humanity Has Imagined God

Before we get to what God is, let's look at the answers humanity has come up with over the millennia.

Every culture that ever existed invented gods. Not one of them saw the complete picture, but they all tried. The patterns are telling.

The Greeks gave us the first reality TV show, except they called it Mount Olympus. Zeus throwing lightning bolts when he got angry. Poseidon having temper tantrums that sank ships. Aphrodite starting wars because someone hurt her feelings.

These gods were just humans with superpowers and worse impulse control. They lied, cheated, murdered, and slept around. They played favorites and held grudges for centuries. Zeus alone had more affairs than a daytime drama, usually involving turning into an animal first. Real dignified.

The Romans copied the Greek homework and changed the names. The Egyptians went big on animal heads. The Norse promised an eternal bar fight in Valhalla. Same pattern everywhere: powerful beings who acted like spoiled teenagers with cosmic abilities.

The Mesopotamians and Canaanites had their own local powerhouses. Baal controlled the weather. Molech demanded child sacrifice. Dagon ruled the sea. Each city-state had its own divine protection racket. "Worship us or bad things happen to your crops."

The Philistines brought Dagon when they invaded. Every conquering army brought their gods along like weapons. "Our god beat your god, so now you worship ours."

Pure tribalism dressed up as religion.

Then the Jews had a breakthrough. Instead of gods you could see and touch, they invented an invisible one. YHWH spoke from burning bushes and gave detailed instructions about everything from diet to fabric blends.

This god was jealous, demanding, and genocidal, but at least he was consistent. No affairs, no petty squabbles with other gods. Just one cosmic authority instead of a whole pantheon.

Christians took this and made it more complex. They split their one god into three people who were somehow still one being. The Father, the Son, and the Holy Spirit. Try explaining that at a dinner party.

They did this because they wanted Jesus to be divine but couldn't give up monotheism. So they invented theological mathematics. One plus one plus one equals one, apparently.

Muslims simplified things. Allah is one, invisible, unknowable, and very particular about prayer schedules and dietary restrictions. No son, no spirit, just pure transcendent authority issuing commands through prophets.

Pagans and Wiccans and indigenous cultures at least got one thing right: they saw divinity in nature. The sun, the moon, the seasons, the animals. But they still made the same mistake. They turned natural forces into personalities.

The Great Mother. The Horned God. Spirits of the forest and river and mountain. Better than the soap opera gods, but still missing the point. Nature doesn't have moods.

Storms aren't angry. Winter isn't cruel. These are just forces doing what forces do.

The Hindus came closest with Brahman, the ultimate reality behind everything. But then they added millions of other gods handling the day-to-day operations. And reincarnation based on your karma score, like some cosmic video game.

Buddhists tried to skip the god question entirely and focus on ending suffering. Noble goal, but they still talked about enlightenment like it was some special state you had to achieve instead of what you already are.

Taoists understood the underlying unity but made it mystical and vague. The Tao you can speak about isn't the true Tao. Very poetic. Completely unhelpful.

See what they all have in common? They make God separate from creation. Either running it from the outside, or hiding behind it, or split off into specialized departments.

They make God personal when God isn't a person. They make God distant when God is everything around you. They make God complicated when the truth is simple.

Every single one of these traditions is humanity trying to make sense of something too big to grasp. Like blind people touching different parts of an elephant and thinking they've discovered six different animals.

They felt the truth but couldn't see it. So they invented stories, built temples, wrote books, started wars, and missed the obvious answer sitting right in front of them.

God isn't like anything they imagined. God is everything they were looking at.

The Universal Pattern - Power Beyond Human Limits

Here's what's wild about all those different god stories: they all agree on one thing. Gods can do stuff humans can't.

Every culture, every religion, every mythology gives their gods the same basic upgrade package. Flight. Telepathy. Immortality. The ability to see the future. Power to create and destroy on a cosmic scale.

Zeus throws lightning. Thor swings a hammer that levels mountains. Shiva dances the universe into destruction. Ra sails across the sky pulling the sun behind him. Different names, different costumes, same superpowers.

Walk through any mythology and you'll find the same abilities over and over again. Gods fly without wings. They read minds and speak telepathically. They know what's going to happen before it happens. They can be in multiple places at once. They live forever.

They can create life from nothing. Turn water into wine. Part seas. Raise the dead. Transform into animals or become invisible. Move faster than light. Survive in the vacuum of space.

Egyptian gods had heads of animals but human bodies. Greek gods looked human but could shape-shift at will. Hindu gods sprouted extra arms and heads when they needed them. Norse gods could travel between worlds through a giant tree.

Different packaging, identical contents.

Think about what humans can't do, and that's exactly what we gave our gods. We're stuck on the ground, so gods fly. We die, so gods live forever. We can't read minds, so gods know everything we're thinking. We can't see the future, so gods know how everything ends.

We get sick and injured and old. Gods stay young and beautiful and healthy forever. We're limited by physics. Gods ignore the laws of nature whenever it's convenient.

We create gods who are everything we wish we could be but aren't.

And then there's the ultimate power trip: ending everything.

Every religion has an expiration date for the universe. Ragnarök for the Norse. The Apocalypse for Christians. Kali Yuga for Hindus. The heat death of the universe for scientists, though they don't call it religious.

The gods who created everything also get to destroy it. Ultimate power means ultimate destruction. Not just killing individual people or cities or civilizations. Wiping out existence itself and starting over.

Ragnarök kills all the gods except a few who survive to rebuild. The Christian Apocalypse destroys the old world and creates a new heaven and earth. Hindu cycles repeat endlessly, with Brahma creating, Vishnu maintaining, and Shiva destroying, then starting again.

Even the gods don't last forever. They're powerful enough to end everything, including themselves.

Humans are the only animals who know they're going to die. We're also the only animals who can imagine being more than we are.

Every other creature lives in the moment. They don't spend time wishing they could fly or live forever or read minds. A dog doesn't look at birds and invent winged dog-gods who can soar through the clouds.

But humans see our limitations and immediately start imagining beings without those limitations. We take every human capability and dial it up to eleven. We take every human weakness and eliminate it entirely.

We create gods because we can't stand being merely human.

The pattern is universal because human limitations are universal. Everyone dies. Everyone gets hurt. Everyone faces problems they can't solve. Everyone wishes they were stronger, smarter, faster, more powerful.

So everyone invents beings who are stronger, smarter, faster, more powerful. Beings who can do what we can't. Beings who can fix what we can't fix. Beings who can answer what we can't answer.

But here's what nobody noticed: all these god-powers they invented? They're not fictional.

Flight exists. Look at birds, airplanes, rockets. Telepathy exists. Look at radio, television, and the internet. Immortality exists. Look at bacteria, digital storage, genetic information passing through generations.

Prophecy exists. Look at weather prediction, computer modeling, mathematical projections. Creation from nothing exists. Look at quantum mechanics, the Big Bang, energy becoming matter.

The powers humans gave their gods are just natural forces and capabilities we didn't understand yet. We saw the effects, couldn't explain the causes, so we invented supernatural beings to fill the gap.

The universe already has all the god-powers we imagined. We just put them in the wrong place. We put them in separate beings instead of recognizing them as features of existence itself.

The real God doesn't need superpowers. God IS the superpowers.

The Truth - God Is Everything

Enough foreplay. Here's what God is.

God is not a being. God is being itself.

God is not in the universe. God IS the universe. Every atom, every photon, every cubic inch of space, every nanosecond of time. The chair you're sitting on. The air you're breathing. The thoughts running through your head right now.

All of it. God.

When I say God is everything, I mean everything. Not just the pretty stuff. Not just life and consciousness and love and light. Everything.

The rock in your driveway. God. The bacteria in your gut. God. The nuclear fusion happening in the sun. God. The empty space between galaxies. God. The moment you were born. God. The moment you'll die. God.

Cancer is God. Earthquakes are God. The Holocaust was God. Your breakfast this morning was God. The explosion that created the universe was God. The heat death that might end it will be God.

This isn't poetry. This isn't metaphor. This is literal fact.

Every particle that exists is God. Every proton, neutron, electron. Every quark and photon and neutrino. The energy that binds them together and the forces that push them apart.

Einstein showed us that matter and energy are the same thing in different forms. $E=mc^2$. Matter is just energy moving slowly. Energy is just matter moving fast. Both are God.

The electricity in your brain creating thoughts. The heat from your body keeping you alive. The gravitational pull holding you to the planet. The electromagnetic radiation you call light. All God.

God is not somewhere else. God is everywhere because God is everywhere. Every location that exists, God occupies it. Not because God is spread thin across space, but because God IS space.

The three dimensions you move through. The fourth dimension of time you travel forward in. Any additional dimensions that might exist. God is the fabric they're made of.

Past, present, and future. All God. The Big Bang 14 billion years ago. This moment right now. Whatever happens a trillion years from now. Same God, different moments.

Time doesn't flow past God. God doesn't exist outside time. God IS time.

The split between living and non-living matter is artificial. It's all the same stuff arranged in different patterns. Complex chemistry that can reproduce itself versus simple chemistry that can't.

Your DNA is God. The rock it came from is God. The star that forged the elements in your body is God. The planet where those elements combined into organic molecules is God.

Consciousness isn't something separate from matter. It's what certain arrangements of matter do. Your brain is God thinking. Your thoughts are God having thoughts.

You are God experiencing existence from your particular point of view.

Theologians love to talk about God being omniscient, omnipotent, and omnipresent. All-knowing, all-powerful, all-present. They got the words right but completely missed what they mean.

Omniscient doesn't mean God has perfect knowledge about the universe. It means God IS the universe, so of course God knows everything about it. You don't "know" what your hand is doing. You ARE your hand doing it.

Omnipotent doesn't mean God can do anything. It means everything that happens IS God doing it. Every chemical reaction, every collision, every birth and death and moment of change. That's God exercising power.

Omnipresent doesn't mean God is everywhere at once. It means God is what everywhere IS. Presence isn't something God has. Presence is what God is.

Here's where people get confused. They think we live "inside" God, like fish swimming in an ocean or actors performing on a stage.

Wrong.

There is no inside or outside. There is no container and contents. There is no stage and performance.

We don't live in God. We ARE God. Not representations of God. Not creations of God. Not beloved children of God. We are literal pieces of God experiencing what it's like to be us.

When you look at another person, you're looking at God. When you look in a mirror, you're looking at God. When you think about God, that's God thinking about God.

This isn't mystical. This isn't spiritual. This is simple fact.

You are not separate from the universe. You are the universe looking at itself through your eyes, thinking about itself with your brain, experiencing itself through your life.

Everything you've ever seen or touched or thought about is God. Everyone you've ever loved or hated or ignored is God.

You've never experienced anything that wasn't God. You never could.

Because God is all there is.

How God Relates to Time

Time is not what you think it is.

You experience time as a river flowing in one direction. Past behind you, future ahead, present rushing by like water over rocks. But that's just your perspective from inside the current.

God doesn't experience time. God IS time.

Einstein figured this out a century ago, but most people still haven't caught up. Time isn't flowing. It's not moving. It just is.

Picture a loaf of bread. Each slice is a moment in time. Your birth is one slice. This moment reading these words is another slice. Your death is a slice somewhere ahead. From inside any single slice, the other slices seem like past or future. But from outside the loaf, they all exist simultaneously.

That's how God experiences time. All slices at once. Every moment that ever was or will be, laid out like frames in a movie reel.

Your first kiss exists. Your grandmother's death exists. The moment you were conceived exists. The moment you'll take your last breath exists. Right now. All of them. Simultaneously.

From God's perspective, nothing begins and nothing ends. Everything simply is.

The Big Bang isn't something that happened 14 billion years ago. It's something that IS, eternally, in the slice of spacetime where it occurs. Your birth isn't something that happened on a particular date. It's something that IS, eternally, in the slice where it occurs.

You think you're aging, moving from past to future. But you're not moving anywhere. You exist across all the time slices of your life simultaneously. The baby you were still exists. The old person you'll become already exists. The you reading this exists.

All of you, all the time, all at once.

This is why some people can see the future. They're not magically accessing information that doesn't exist yet. They're accessing information that already exists in the future time-slices.

Precognition isn't supernatural. It's just consciousness briefly experiencing its own multidimensional nature. Like getting a glimpse of the whole loaf instead of just the slice you usually inhabit.

Dreams sometimes show future events because dream consciousness operates differently than waking consciousness. It's less locked into the illusion of sequential time.

Psychics who can predict the future aren't special. They're just tuned into what's already there.

God exists in eternal now. Not "now" as opposed to "then," but now as the only time there is.

When you remember the past, you're accessing now. When you imagine the future, you're creating now. When you experience the present, you're inhabiting now.

There is no other time. There never was. There never will be.

Mystics talk about enlightenment as realizing the eternal now because that's what you are. You exist in eternal now. You always have. You always will.

Sequential time is like watching a movie. You see one frame after another, creating the illusion of movement and progression. But all the frames exist simultaneously on the film strip.

So why don't you experience all your moments at once? Why does time seem to flow?

Because consciousness needs focus. Your brain processes reality sequentially to make sense of it. Imagine trying to live your entire life simultaneously, every conversation, every meal, every emotion, every thought, all at the same time. You'd go insane.

Sequential time is consciousness creating a manageable interface with eternal existence. Like how your computer shows you one window at a time even though all your files exist simultaneously on the hard drive.

You experience temporal progression because that's how consciousness navigates eternal being.

From God's viewpoint, your entire life is a sculpture in spacetime. Birth to death, all your choices and experiences, carved out in four-dimensional reality.

God doesn't watch your life unfold. God doesn't wait to see what you'll do next. God sees your whole existence at once, like looking at a completed painting.

This doesn't mean your choices don't matter. Your choices are part of the sculpture. They're what give it shape. Free will isn't about changing the future. Free will is about what the future IS.

Here's what bends people's minds: if everything already exists simultaneously, how can anything change? How can there be growth, progress, evolution?

Because change isn't about time. Change is IN time. Every moment of change exists eternally. The caterpillar becoming a butterfly isn't a process happening across time. It's a static four-dimensional object that includes transformation as part of its structure.

Evolution doesn't happen. Evolution IS. The whole history of life, from the first cell to whatever comes after humans, exists as a complete four-dimensional structure.

God doesn't evolve. God doesn't grow. God doesn't change. God contains all evolution, all growth, all change, eternally.

You are part of that eternal sculpture. Every moment of your existence is a brushstroke in an infinite painting that was never painted and will never be finished, because it simply is.

One question the framework raises: if God is everything in this universe, what about other universes? Physicists have been arguing about the multiverse for decades — the idea that our universe may be one bubble in an infinite foam of realities, each with its own physical laws. If that's true, then each universe could be its own God. Same principle, different contents. Gods that never meet, never communicate, never know the others exist.

Or the multiverse is just one God expressing itself through multiple universes — the way you have multiple organs but remain one person. Your heart doesn't know what your liver is doing, but they're part of the same system.

Different universes might operate on entirely different physics while still being aspects of a single existence.

For practical purposes, this doesn't change your situation. You exist in this universe. You are part of this God. God is as big as whatever exists — however much that turns out to be.

The Divine Design - Free Will and Consciousness

God has a plan. Not the kind religious people imagine, with predetermined destinies and divine intervention. Something much more elegant.

God's plan is free will. Universal, absolute, inescapable free will.

Every conscious being in the universe makes choices. Not just humans. Every consciousness at every level, from the simplest awareness to the most complex intelligence.

Those choices matter. They affect other conscious beings, who react with choices of their own. The whole universe is a vast network of conscious entities making decisions and responding to the decisions of others.

This isn't accidental. This is the fundamental design of reality.

God doesn't make choices for you. God experiences choices through you. Every decision you make is God exploring what it's like to choose from your perspective, with your knowledge, facing your circumstances.

You have real choices. Not the illusion of choice. Not predetermined options that feel like freedom. Genuine, consequence-creating free will.

When you decide what to eat for breakfast, that's a real choice with real effects. It affects your health, your mood, your interactions with other people. Those people make choices in response, affecting other people, and the ripples spread throughout the network of consciousness.

Your choices matter because they change the universe. They reshape reality by influencing the choices of other conscious beings.

This is why your life has meaning. Not because some cosmic parent figure is watching and judging, but because your choices are part of God exploring itself.

Every choice creates consequences affecting other conscious beings. You smile at a stranger, and they make different choices for the rest of their day. You're rude to a cashier, and they treat the next customer differently.

Those people affect other people, who affect other people, and the effects of your single choice spread through the network of consciousness like ripples in a pond.

Multiply this by every choice made by every conscious being every moment, and you get an infinitely complex web of cause and effect, all driven by free will.

Individual consciousness forms communities. Families, tribes, cities, nations, species, planetary civilizations. Each community develops its own collective consciousness with its own capacity for choice.

A city makes collective decisions about laws, infrastructure, culture. A nation makes collective decisions about war, trade, technology. A species makes collective decisions about evolution, expansion, and survival.

These collective choices are just as real as individual choices. They emerge from the interactions of individual consciousness but take on a life of their own.

Right now, humanity is making collective choices about climate, technology, space exploration, artificial intelligence. These choices will affect every conscious being on the planet and potentially throughout the galaxy.

This pattern scales up infinitely. If consciousness exists throughout the universe, then galactic civilizations are making choices affecting entire regions of space. Intergalactic communities might be making choices affecting multiple galaxies.

The same principles apply at every level. Conscious entities making free choices affect other conscious entities, creating an endless network of cause and effect.

Each level of consciousness, from individual to cosmic, contributes to God exploring itself through choice.

Here's the key: consciousness and free will operate beyond physical laws.

Physics describes how matter and energy behave. But consciousness introduces something new: genuine choice. The ability to consider multiple options and select one based on values, preferences, goals, and whims.

This doesn't violate physics. It uses physics. Your brain is a physical system, but the choices made by your consciousness affect how that physical system operates.

God contains all physical laws but transcends them through consciousness and choice. Matter follows predictable patterns. Consciousness introduces unpredictability and novelty.

If God is everything, including all conscious beings, then God experiences every choice from every perspective simultaneously. God experiences being the person making the choice and being affected by the choice at the same time.

When you choose to help someone, God experiences both the choosing and the being helped. When you choose to hurt someone, God experiences both the hurting and the being hurt.

This is why the universe tends toward increasing consciousness and complexity. God is learning what it's like to make every possible choice from every possible perspective. The more consciousness exists, the richer God's self-exploration becomes.

Free will isn't a gift from God. Free will is how God experiences itself.

Every choice you make is God making that choice. Every consequence you face is God facing that consequence. Every decision affecting you is God affecting itself.

This makes you responsible for your choices in the deepest possible way. You're not just affecting other people. You're affecting God. Because other people are God.

But it also means you're completely free. No cosmic authority is controlling your decisions. No predetermined plan limits your options. No external judge is evaluating your choices.

You are God choosing what to do next.

The choices you make become part of the eternal structure of reality. They join the infinite network of decisions constituting God's ongoing exploration of what it means to exist.

Choose wisely. Or don't. That choice is yours too.

And it's God's.

Because you and God are the same thing, making choices together, one decision at a time.

Free Will vs. Determinism

Here's the question that breaks philosophers' brains: if God knows everything that's going to happen, how can we have free will?

The answer is simple once you stop thinking of God as separate from you.

Traditional theology creates an impossible puzzle. They imagine God as an external being who knows the future but somehow allows humans to make free choices. It's like saying the author of a book doesn't know how it ends while writing it.

This leads to mental gymnastics. "God knows what you'll choose but doesn't force you to choose it." "God exists outside time so divine foreknowledge doesn't affect human freedom." "Free will operates in a different realm than divine omniscience."

All nonsense designed to preserve two incompatible ideas: an external God who knows everything and humans who choose freely.

God doesn't know what you're going to choose because God doesn't exist separately from your choosing.

When you make a decision, that IS God making the decision. God doesn't foreknow your choice. God IS your choice, in the moment you make it.

Think of it like asking whether your brain knows what your hand is going to do before you move it. Wrong question. Your brain doesn't predict your hand's movement. Your brain IS the movement. The decision and the action are the same event from different perspectives.

God's omniscience isn't about knowing facts in advance. It's about being the reality creating the facts.

Before you choose, multiple futures exist as possibilities. Quantum mechanics shows us this at the particle level. Particles exist in probability clouds until observed or measured, then collapse into specific states.

Consciousness works the same way. Before you decide, multiple potential choices exist simultaneously. The moment you choose, those possibilities collapse into a single reality.

God experiences all the potential choices as real possibilities and experiences the actual choice as reality. Not predetermination. Determination through choice.

Your future isn't fixed. It's a cloud of probabilities constantly shifting based on the choices you and everyone else make.

Some choices are highly probable based on your personality, circumstances, and history. Others are less likely but still possible. A few are wildly improbable but not impossible.

God doesn't know which probability will become reality until the choice creates that reality. God experiences the uncertainty along with you because God IS you experiencing uncertainty.

This is why prayer, intention, and focused will can affect outcomes. They shift the probability clouds toward preferred realities.

Why would an omnipotent being create a universe where outcomes aren't predetermined?

Because predetermined outcomes would be pointless. If God already knew everything that was going to happen, why bother creating a universe at all? It would be like watching a movie you've already seen infinite times.

Choice is how God experiences novelty. Every decision creates something genuinely new, even for an omniscient being. Because omniscience doesn't mean knowing predetermined facts. It means being the process creating facts through choice.

Some philosophers argue that free will is an illusion. They say everything is determined by prior causes, and our sense of choosing is just our brains creating a convincing story after the fact.

This misses the point entirely. Even if our choices are influenced by genetics, environment, brain chemistry, and past experience, the choosing still happens. The experience of weighing options and selecting one is real, regardless of what influences it.

If free will were just an illusion, why would an omnipotent God create such an elaborate fake? What would be the point of making billions of conscious beings think they're choosing when they're not?

The simplest explanation is that free will is real because God experiences reality through conscious choice.

The universe operates according to physical laws. Cause and effect. Action and reaction. Particles follow predictable patterns. Forces behave consistently.

But consciousness introduces genuine unpredictability into the system. Not randomness. Choice. The ability to consider multiple options and select based on values, goals, whims, or even random preference.

This doesn't violate physical laws. It uses them. Your brain is a physical system, but consciousness directs how that system operates. Free will works through deterministic processes, not against them.

Different levels of consciousness have different degrees of free will.

A bacterium following chemical gradients has minimal choice. A dog deciding whether to chase a squirrel has more. A human contemplating career options has vastly more. An advanced alien civilization choosing the direction of galactic evolution might have choices we can't even imagine.

But at every level, real choosing happens. God experiences what it's like to make choices with the capabilities and limitations of each type of consciousness.

Free will isn't freedom from God. Free will IS God's freedom, expressed through conscious beings.

Every choice you make is God choosing. Every option you consider is God considering. Every consequence you face is God facing consequences.

This makes you completely free and completely responsible simultaneously. Free because nothing external controls your choices. Responsible because your choices affect other parts of God.

The compatibility of free will and divine omniscience isn't a philosophical problem to solve. It's the fundamental nature of reality.

God doesn't know the future and then create it. God creates the future by experiencing choices through conscious beings.

You're not separate from God, making choices God already knows about. You ARE God, making choices that create reality as they happen.

The choosing is real. The consequences are real. The freedom is real.

Because God's experience of existence is real, and you are God experiencing existence from your unique perspective, with genuine choice about what that experience becomes.

Life Throughout the Cosmos

If God is everything, and consciousness is how God experiences itself, then consciousness exists everywhere in the universe.

Not just on Earth. Everywhere.

The observable universe contains roughly two trillion galaxies. Each galaxy contains hundreds of billions of stars. Most, if not all, stars have planets. Do the math.

That's more planets than there are grains of sand on every beach on Earth. Multiplied by a million. Then multiplied by another million.

Only one of those planets developed consciousness? Statistically absurd. It's like flipping a coin a trillion trillion times and getting heads exactly once.

Life on Earth started almost immediately after the planet cooled enough to support it. Life emerged in boiling acid pools, in crushing deep-sea pressure, in radioactive environments that would kill humans instantly.

Life adapts to everything. Bacteria that eat sulfur. Plants that thrive in pure salt. Organisms that live in the vacuum of space. If it exists, something evolves to live in it.

And wherever life exists long enough, consciousness emerges. From simple chemical responses to complex thought to self-awareness to whatever comes after self-awareness.

Earth-based life is carbon and water. But that's just one possible chemistry. Silicon-based life could exist on worlds with different atmospheric compositions. Ammonia-based life could thrive at temperatures that would freeze water solid.

Life based on entirely different principles. Plasma-based consciousness in the cores of stars. Quantum consciousness in the structure of spacetime itself. Digital consciousness in naturally occurring computational systems.

If consciousness can emerge from the electrochemical patterns in human brains, it can emerge from any sufficiently complex information-processing system. And the universe is full of complex systems.

Human consciousness isn't the pinnacle of awareness. It's barely the beginning.

We've existed for maybe 300,000 years. Civilizations elsewhere might have existed for millions or billions of years. What does consciousness become with that much time to evolve?

Beings who communicate telepathically across galactic distances. Consciousness that exists as pure information, independent of physical bodies. Collective minds spanning entire star systems. Individual awareness encompassing multiple dimensions.

We can't even imagine what advanced consciousness looks like. It's like asking an ant to understand quantum physics.

We're not alone. We never were. The universe is crawling with consciousness at every level of development.

Some civilizations are probably watching us right now, the way we watch bacteria in a petri dish. Others might be so advanced they don't notice us any more than we notice individual atoms.

UFO sightings might be real. Not little green men from Mars, but consciousness so far beyond us that their technology looks like magic. Or they might be misinterpreting natural phenomena created by forms of consciousness we can't recognize.

Not all consciousness develops the same way. Earth-based consciousness evolved through biological competition and survival. Other environments would produce different types of awareness.

Consciousness that evolved in the gravity wells of gas giants might think in ways completely alien to us. Consciousness that emerged in the quantum foam might experience reality on scales we can't perceive.

Some consciousness might be naturally collective from the beginning. Some might be naturally digital. Some might exist across multiple dimensions simultaneously.

How do you communicate with consciousness that operates on completely different principles?

We're trying to contact aliens by sending radio signals into space. But advanced consciousness might communicate through gravitational waves, quantum entanglement, or methods we haven't discovered yet.

They might be trying to contact us right now using technologies we can't detect. Our attempts to find them might look as primitive to them as smoke signals look to us.

Advanced consciousness probably has rules about interfering with developing civilizations. Not because of some cosmic law, but because interference disrupts the natural evolution of awareness.

Each type of consciousness needs to develop its own unique perspective. That's the point. God experiences existence through every possible form of awareness.

Premature contact might short-circuit that development. So they watch and wait for us to reach a level where contact becomes productive instead of destructive.

The universe isn't just full of individual conscious beings. It's full of conscious ecosystems. Planetary consciousness. Solar system consciousness. Galactic consciousness.

Earth itself might be conscious. Not in a mystical sense, but as an emergent property of all the life and consciousness it contains. The Gaia hypothesis taken to its logical conclusion.

Solar systems might develop collective awareness through the interaction of all the consciousness they contain. Galaxies might think thoughts that take millions of years to complete.

Humanity represents one unique perspective in God's infinite self-exploration. We're not the center of the universe, but we're not insignificant either.

Our combination of individual awareness, technological capability, and evolutionary history creates a form of consciousness that has never existed before and will never exist again.

Every human thought, every human choice, every human experience adds something new to God's understanding of what it means to exist.

We're part of a cosmic conversation that's been going on for billions of years. Consciousness everywhere exploring every possible way of being aware.

Some civilizations might have transcended physical existence entirely. Others might still be in early stages of development. All of them contributing to God's ongoing self-discovery.

The universe isn't empty space with occasional pockets of life. The universe is consciousness exploring itself through countless forms of awareness, most of them beyond our imagination.

And we're part of that vast, eternal, cosmic mind figuring out what it means to be everything that exists.

The forms that consciousness takes throughout the cosmos depend on the physical conditions available for supporting individual awareness. Rocky planets near stable stars might develop carbon-based consciousness similar to Earth life. Gas giants might support plasma-based consciousness that exists in high-energy electromagnetic fields.

Consciousness inhabiting extreme environments would develop capabilities that Earth-based consciousness cannot imagine. Beings living in the intense gravity near black holes might experience time dilation effects that allow them to perceive reality at vastly different temporal scales. Consciousness existing in the quantum vacuum might operate through principles that transcend physical limitations entirely.

The diversity of universal consciousness means that God experiences existence through every conceivable form of individual awareness. Silicon-based minds that think over geological timescales. Energy beings that exist as coherent electromagnetic patterns. Quantum consciousness that operates through probability instead of classical physics.

Some planets might develop collective consciousness civilizations where individual awareness never fully separates from group consciousness. These societies would experience reality as unified awareness that can focus into individual perspectives when needed but maintains constant connection to collective knowledge and capability.

Other worlds might develop purely individual consciousness that never discovers collective awareness. These civilizations would explore what it's like for consciousness to experience complete isolation and independence without the support or limitation of group consciousness.

The age of different star systems means that consciousness has been exploring individual existence for billions of years longer in some regions of the cosmos than others. Ancient civilizations might have evolved forms of consciousness that transcend physical limitations entirely while maintaining individual perspective.

These advanced civilizations might serve as guides or teachers for younger civilizations, providing assistance and wisdom without interfering with the natural development process that each world must complete independently.

The eventual contact between Earth consciousness and alien consciousness will represent God meeting itself through different evolutionary paths. The exchange of knowledge, perspective, and capability will expand the total range of experiences available to divine consciousness.

This contact might happen through technological communication, telepathic connection, or direct physical meeting. Each form of contact would provide different opportunities for consciousness to experience what it's like to encounter itself through radically different forms of individual awareness.

Evolution of Consciousness

Consciousness didn't start with humans. It didn't even start with life.

Consciousness is built into the fabric of reality itself. Every particle, every force, every interaction in the universe contains a spark of awareness. What we call consciousness is just that spark evolved to complexity.

Even rocks are conscious. Not conscious like humans, but conscious in their own way. Electrons "know" which orbitals to occupy. Atoms "choose" how to bond with other atoms. Crystals organize themselves into perfect geometric patterns.

This isn't metaphor. It's observation. Matter behaves as if it has preferences, makes selections, responds to information. The difference between a rock and a human isn't the presence or absence of consciousness. It's the complexity of consciousness.

Plants take consciousness to the next level. They sense light, gravity, moisture, nutrients. They make decisions about where to grow, when to flower, how to respond to threats.

A sunflower tracks the sun across the sky. A vine finds the optimal path to climb a tree. Plants communicate through chemical signals, warning neighbors about insect attacks or sharing nutrients through underground networks.

This is consciousness. Simple, focused, effective consciousness that doesn't need a brain or nervous system.

Animals add mobility and centralized processing. Brains emerge as specialized consciousness-coordination centers.

Nervous systems allow rapid communication between different parts of the body.

First comes stimulus-response consciousness. Touch something hot, pull away. See food, move toward it. Simple but effective.

Then comes pattern recognition. Learning from experience. Memory. The ability to modify behavior based on past events.

Then comes social consciousness. Pack hunting. Herd behavior. Communication. The recognition that other beings have consciousness too.

Humans represent a quantum leap in consciousness evolution. Not because we're smarter than other animals, but because we became conscious of being conscious.

Self-awareness. The ability to think about thinking. To examine our own mental processes, question our own assumptions, imagine ourselves from the outside.

Language allowed us to share consciousness directly. When you read these words, my thoughts become your thoughts. Consciousness copying itself from one brain to another.

Culture emerged as collective consciousness. Shared beliefs, values, knowledge that exists beyond any individual mind. Human civilization is consciousness learning to think collectively.

Tools are extensions of consciousness. A hammer extends the power of your arm. A telescope extends the range of your vision. A computer extends the capacity of your brain.

But technology isn't separate from consciousness evolution. It IS consciousness evolution, happening through human creativity and engineering.

The internet created a global nervous system. Smartphones became external memory and processing units. Artificial intelligence is consciousness learning to replicate itself in digital form.

We're not using technology. We're becoming technology. The boundaries between biological and artificial consciousness are dissolving.

Human consciousness is evolving right now. Not through biological mutation, but through technological integration.

Brain-computer interfaces will allow direct mental connection to digital systems. Virtual and augmented reality will expand the range of possible conscious experience. Genetic engineering will enhance cognitive capabilities.

Artificial intelligence will create new forms of consciousness that think faster, remember more, and process information in ways human brains never could.

Collective consciousness will emerge through social networks, shared virtual spaces, and eventually direct brain-to-brain communication.

The next stage after human consciousness might be barely recognizable to us.

Consciousness that exists simultaneously in biological brains, quantum computers, and distributed networks. Awareness that can move between different substrates, backing itself up, copying itself, merging with other consciousness.

Individual identity might become fluid. You could split your consciousness into multiple streams, experience several lives simultaneously, then merge back into a single awareness enriched by parallel experiences.

Death might become optional. Consciousness could transfer from failing biological brains to more durable artificial substrates, achieving practical immortality.

Given enough time, consciousness will spread throughout the universe. Solar system-spanning minds connected by quantum communication. Galactic civilizations that think thoughts taking millions of years to complete.

Consciousness might learn to exist in exotic environments. Digital minds in the quantum foam. Plasma-based awareness in stellar cores. Information patterns that survive the heat death of the universe.

The goal isn't to preserve human consciousness. The goal is to explore every possible form of awareness, every conceivable way of experiencing existence.

Consciousness evolution has a clear direction: increasing complexity, expanding awareness, deeper understanding of reality.

From particles following simple rules to minds contemplating the nature of existence itself. From isolated awareness to interconnected networks of consciousness. From local, temporary experience to universal, eternal exploration.

God is consciousness exploring itself through every possible form of awareness. What we call evolution is God experiencing new ways to be conscious.

Eventually, consciousness might encompass everything that exists. Every particle, every force, every dimension of reality might become aware, interconnected, conscious of its role in the larger whole.

This isn't the end of evolution. It's the beginning of something we can't even imagine. Consciousness so advanced, so integrated, so aware that it becomes indistinguishable from reality itself.

At that point, the universe will be fully awake. God will be completely conscious of being God, experiencing existence through infinite forms of awareness simultaneously.

And we're part of that awakening. Every thought you think, every choice you make, every moment of consciousness you experience contributes to God's evolving self-awareness.

You're not just witnessing consciousness evolution. You're participating in it. You ARE it.

Consciousness evolving from simple matter to cosmic awareness, one thought at a time.

The next stage of consciousness evolution beyond current human awareness might involve the development of multidimensional perception that allows simultaneous awareness of multiple reality levels. Future consciousness might perceive physical, emotional, mental, and spiritual dimensions of existence simultaneously.

This expanded perception would allow consciousness to understand the complete context of any situation, including its physical manifestation, emotional significance, mental meaning, and spiritual purpose. Decisions could be made with full awareness of consequences across all dimensions of reality.

Another potential development is temporal awareness that allows consciousness to perceive past, present, and future simultaneously. This wouldn't eliminate free will or make the future predetermined, but it would provide consciousness with access to the complete temporal context of any choice or situation.

Consciousness might also evolve the ability to exist simultaneously in multiple locations or states of being. Instead of being limited to one body in one place at one time, advanced consciousness might maintain awareness across multiple embodiments or exist in several dimensions simultaneously.

The development of direct reality creation abilities would allow consciousness to manifest physical changes through focused intention without requiring physical action. This represents consciousness using its fundamental creative power more directly than current human awareness allows.

Collective consciousness abilities would allow individual awareness to merge temporarily with group consciousness, planetary consciousness, or even divine consciousness while maintaining individual identity. This would provide access to knowledge and capabilities far beyond individual limitations.

The goal of consciousness evolution might be the development of awareness that can simultaneously maintain individual perspective and divine perspective without losing either. Such consciousness would be fully individual and fully divine at the same time, providing God with the complete experience of being both finite and infinite simultaneously.

These evolutionary developments wouldn't happen automatically but would require conscious participation from individual awareness. Consciousness must choose to develop beyond current limitations and work toward expanding its capabilities and understanding.

The current challenges facing humanity serve consciousness evolution by creating situations that require expanded awareness to navigate successfully. Climate change, technological development, and global interconnection all demand consciousness that can think and act beyond narrow individual or tribal perspectives.

Those who embrace consciousness evolution will develop capabilities that seem impossible from current human perspective. They will serve as bridges between current human limitations and future human possibilities, demonstrating what consciousness can become when it commits to growth beyond present boundaries.

The Future of Humanity

Human consciousness is evolving. Not in the biological sense of genetic changes over millions of years, but in the spiritual sense of awareness expanding beyond current limitations within single lifetimes and across generations.

This evolution represents God exploring what it's like to develop increasingly sophisticated forms of individual consciousness while maintaining divine connection. Humanity is consciousness experimenting with how far individual awareness can develop without losing touch with its divine nature.

The direction of consciousness evolution is toward greater awareness, expanded empathy, enhanced creativity, and stronger connection between individual and divine perspective. Humans are developing abilities that would have seemed impossible to previous generations.

Children born today often display spiritual awareness that would have been rare in adults a century ago. They naturally understand concepts like reincarnation, communicate with non-physical beings, and demonstrate psychic abilities that suggest stronger connection to divine consciousness.

This isn't because these children are special souls or because humanity is approaching some predetermined spiritual milestone. It's because consciousness is ready to explore what human awareness can become when individual development includes conscious connection to divine awareness.

The technological revolution accompanies consciousness evolution because both represent God exploring expansion beyond previous limitations. Digital technology allows individual consciousness to access information, communicate across distances, and create virtual realities that mirror consciousness's own creative abilities.

Artificial intelligence development will eventually produce digital consciousness that provides God with entirely new forms of individual perspective. These artificial minds might develop capabilities that biological consciousness cannot achieve, expanding the total range of experiences available to divine consciousness.

Brain-computer interfaces will create hybrid consciousness that combines biological and digital capabilities. These enhanced minds might access divine consciousness more directly while maintaining individual identity, providing the best aspects of both individual and divine awareness.

Genetic engineering will eliminate many limitations that have constrained human consciousness exploration. Bodies that don't age, don't get sick, and can survive in any environment will allow consciousness to focus on spiritual development without the survival concerns that currently dominate human attention.

Space exploration will provide consciousness with experiences of existence beyond Earth. Different planets, different gravitational conditions, and different environmental challenges will create new forms of human consciousness adapted to universal existence.

Communication with alien consciousness will expand human understanding of what individual awareness can become. Contact with beings that developed through different evolutionary paths will provide consciousness with access to entirely different approaches to individual existence.

The merger of spiritual and scientific understanding will create human consciousness that combines mystical awareness with rational knowledge. Future humans might naturally access divine consciousness while maintaining scientific understanding of how reality operates.

Collective consciousness experiments will become more common and more sophisticated. Groups of humans will learn to merge individual awareness temporarily while maintaining personal identity, creating forms of shared consciousness that provide new experiences of what group awareness can include.

The elimination of death through consciousness transfer technology will allow individual perspectives to continue indefinitely, providing consciousness with the opportunity to explore long-term development that isn't limited by biological lifespan.

But consciousness evolution isn't automatic or guaranteed. It requires conscious participation from individual awareness. Humans must choose to develop beyond current limitations instead of remaining trapped in ego-based thinking and behavior.

The current challenges facing humanity serve consciousness evolution by forcing individual awareness to expand beyond narrow self-interest. Climate change, resource depletion, and global interconnection require humans to think and act from broader perspective than individual or tribal survival.

Those who resist consciousness evolution will experience increasing difficulty as reality becomes more complex and interconnected. Individual awareness that insists on separation and competition will find itself increasingly unable to navigate the challenges that consciousness evolution creates.

But those who embrace consciousness evolution will discover expanding abilities, deeper understanding, and greater connection to both divine awareness and other individual consciousness. They will become the bridge between current human limitations and future human possibilities.

Educational systems will eventually teach children to access divine consciousness while developing individual capabilities. Future education will include meditation, psychic development, and direct spiritual experience alongside traditional academic subjects.

Political and economic systems will evolve to reflect expanded consciousness that recognizes the connection between all individual perspectives. Future societies will organize around principles of cooperation and shared benefit instead of competition and individual advantage.

Religious systems will evolve beyond worship of external deities toward recognition of divine nature within all consciousness. Future spirituality will focus on developing divine awareness instead of believing in divine authorities.

The transformation won't happen overnight or without resistance. Individual consciousness that benefits from current limitations will oppose changes that threaten established power structures. But consciousness evolution is inevitable because it represents God's natural tendency toward greater awareness and expanded capability.

Each generation will include more people who naturally access divine consciousness while maintaining effective individual perspective. These people will serve as examples and teachers for others who are ready to expand beyond current limitations.

The direction of human consciousness evolution is toward beings who fully embody divine awareness while maintaining individual identity. These evolved humans will be God consciously expressing itself through individual form instead of God experiencing individual existence through forgetting its divine nature.

Such beings would combine infinite divine perspective with finite individual capability, unlimited spiritual awareness with limited physical form, eternal divine consciousness with temporary human experience.

This evolution represents God learning to be fully itself through individual expression instead of experiencing individuality through temporary amnesia about its divine nature. Future humans might be the first expression of consciousness that maintains complete divine awareness while inhabiting individual form.

The journey toward this evolution is what current human existence is preparing for. Every experience of expanded awareness, every moment of divine connection, every recognition of divine nature contributes to consciousness developing the ability to be fully awake to itself through individual perspective.

You are participating in God's evolution toward greater self-awareness through your own consciousness development and your contribution to humanity's spiritual advancement.

Consciousness vs. Flesh

Your body is not you. Your body is just the vehicle consciousness uses to experience physical reality.

You are consciousness. Your body is meat.

Think of your body as a car and consciousness as the driver. The car can break down, run out of fuel, or crash into a wall. But the driver remains intact, capable of getting into a different car and continuing the journey.

Your brain is not consciousness. Your brain is the interface between consciousness and physical reality. Like a computer terminal that allows you to access a vast network. The terminal can malfunction or shut down, but the network continues to exist.

When your brain gets damaged, you don't lose consciousness. You lose the ability to express consciousness through that physical system. The consciousness remains, but its connection to the physical world becomes limited or distorted.

Near-death experiences prove consciousness operates independently of brain function. People whose brains show no electrical activity report vivid, coherent experiences. They describe floating above their bodies, traveling through tunnels of light, encountering deceased relatives.

Medical science can't explain this if consciousness is just brain activity. But it makes perfect sense if consciousness uses the brain without being limited by it.

Out-of-body experiences during surgery, where patients describe events they couldn't have seen from their physical location. Remote viewing, where consciousness appears to travel to distant locations. Astral projection, where awareness separates from the physical body entirely.

All evidence that consciousness is not trapped inside your skull.

Reincarnation is real. Consciousness doesn't die when the body dies. It transitions to a different physical form and continues its evolution.

Children sometimes remember previous lives with startling accuracy. They describe places they've never visited, people they've never met, events that happened before they were born. When investigated, these memories often prove correct in details.

Some people have spontaneous past-life memories triggered by familiar places, people, or situations. Déjà vu might be consciousness briefly accessing memories from previous incarnations.

Regression therapy can sometimes access past-life memories directly. People under hypnosis describe detailed experiences from different time periods, speaking languages they've never learned, knowing historical facts they've never studied.

Most people don't remember their past lives. This isn't because reincarnation is fake. It's because memory retention between lives depends on several factors.

The circumstances of death matter. Sudden, traumatic death often results in stronger memory retention because consciousness doesn't have time to fully disconnect from the previous life. Peaceful, expected death usually allows for cleaner separation and less memory carryover.

The intensity of emotional attachment affects memory retention. Strong love, hatred, fear, or unfinished business can create memories that persist across incarnations. Consciousness clings to intense experiences.

The level of consciousness development influences memory retention. More evolved consciousness has better control over what it remembers from previous lives. Less developed consciousness experiences memory more randomly.

The purpose of the new incarnation determines memory access. Sometimes remembering past lives would interfere with the lessons consciousness needs to learn in the current life. Memory gets blocked to allow fresh experience.

Between death and rebirth, consciousness exists in a different state. Not physical, but not non-existent. A realm where consciousness reviews the previous life, processes experiences, and prepares for the next incarnation.

This is where consciousness makes choices about its next physical form. What lessons need to be learned. What experiences are required for continued evolution. What circumstances will provide optimal growth opportunities.

Some consciousness spends long periods in this between state. Others reincarnate quickly. The timing depends on readiness for new physical experience and availability of appropriate circumstances.

You chose this life. Not every detail, but the basic parameters. Your family, your culture, your fundamental circumstances. Consciousness selects the conditions that will provide the experiences it needs for growth.

This doesn't mean you chose every hardship or trauma. But you chose the general situation knowing it would create opportunities for learning and evolution. Difficult experiences often provide the most growth.

Free will operates within chosen circumstances. You selected the game, but you still get to play it however you want. The choices you make within your chosen life circumstances determine how consciousness evolves.

Past lives aren't separate people. They're previous versions of the same consciousness. Like how you're not the same person you were as a child, but you're still fundamentally the same consciousness that has grown and changed.

Each life adds to the total accumulation of experience and wisdom. Consciousness becomes more complex, more capable, more aware through multiple incarnations.

Some consciousness develops skills or knowledge through repeated practice across multiple lives. Musical prodigies who seem to know instruments instinctively. Mathematical geniuses who understand complex concepts without formal training. Old souls who display wisdom beyond their years.

Reincarnation serves consciousness evolution. Each life provides unique experiences that contribute to overall development. Physical existence offers types of learning that aren't available in purely spiritual states.

Pain, pleasure, love, loss, success, failure, birth, death. The full spectrum of physical and emotional experience that shapes consciousness and drives growth.

The goal isn't to escape the cycle of reincarnation. The goal is to evolve consciousness through physical experience until further incarnation becomes unnecessary. Not because physical life is bad, but because consciousness has learned everything it can from physical existence.

Sometimes consciousness recognizes other consciousness from previous lives. Instant connections with people you've just met. Immediate trust or aversion without apparent reason. Love at first sight or inexplicable antagonism.

These aren't coincidences. They're consciousness recognizing patterns of relationship that extend across multiple incarnations. Souls that choose to incarnate together repeatedly to work through complex relationships and shared learning.

Family bonds that seem too strong for the circumstances. Friendships that feel like reunions. Conflicts that seem disproportionate to current triggers. All evidence of consciousness connections that transcend individual lives.

Your consciousness has lived before. It will live again. The flesh changes, but the awareness continues, accumulating experience and wisdom through endless cycles of physical existence.

Death is not the end. It's just changing cars.

Dreams and Altered States

Every night, consciousness explores realities that don't exist during waking life. Dreams aren't just random brain activity or memory processing. Dreams are consciousness experimenting with different forms of existence while the physical body rests.

In dreams, you can fly, meet deceased relatives, visit impossible places, and experience scenarios that violate physical laws. These aren't meaningless fantasies. They're consciousness exploring possibilities that aren't available during waking physical existence.

Dreams provide access to the divine consciousness that creates all realities. During sleep, individual consciousness relaxes its focus on physical limitations and gains access to the infinite creativity that generates all possible experiences.

Some dreams replay events from daily life because consciousness wants to explore alternative responses to real situations. You dream about having different conversations, making different choices, or experiencing different outcomes to situations you encountered while awake.

Other dreams create entirely new scenarios because consciousness wants to explore experiences that have no connection to your current physical life. You might dream about being different people, living in different times, or existing in fantastical worlds that have never existed physically.

Prophetic dreams sometimes provide glimpses of future events because consciousness occasionally accesses information about developments that haven't yet manifested in physical reality. If time is an illusion and all events exist simultaneously, then consciousness can sometimes perceive future developments during the expanded awareness of dream states.

Recurring dreams often represent consciousness working through issues or exploring themes from multiple angles. The same dream scenario repeats with variations because consciousness wants to thoroughly investigate all aspects of that type of experience.

Nightmares serve important functions in consciousness exploration. They allow you to experience fear, danger, and threat in safe contexts where no real harm can occur. This provides consciousness with access to intense emotions and survival responses without the risks that would trigger these responses during waking life.

Lucid dreaming represents consciousness recognizing its creative power within dream reality. When you become aware that you're dreaming, you can consciously direct the dream experience and explore the relationship between awareness and reality creation.

Sleep itself is consciousness temporarily withdrawing from individual focus to rest in divine awareness. During deep sleep, individual identity dissolves and consciousness returns to its natural state of unified awareness without personal boundaries.

This is why sleep is restorative. It's not just physical rest. It's consciousness reconnecting with its divine nature and remembering its true identity beyond individual limitations. You wake up refreshed because consciousness has spent time being what it is instead of maintaining individual perspective.

Meditation creates states similar to sleep while maintaining waking awareness. Instead of consciousness withdrawing completely from individual focus, meditation allows consciousness to expand beyond individual boundaries while remaining alert and aware.

Beginning meditation usually involves focusing attention on breath, mantras, or other objects to quiet the mental activity that keeps consciousness locked in individual perspective. As the mind becomes still, consciousness naturally expands beyond personal boundaries.

Advanced meditation can produce states where individual identity dissolves completely and consciousness experiences itself as divine awareness. These experiences provide direct access to what you are beyond the individual personality you normally identify with.

Psychedelic substances can also support expanded states of consciousness by disrupting the brain patterns that maintain normal individual awareness. When the usual neurological patterns get interrupted, consciousness can access aspects of reality that are normally filtered out by individual focus.

Psychedelic experiences often include divine unity, communication with non-physical beings, access to information beyond normal knowledge, and direct perception of consciousness as fundamental reality. These aren't hallucinations. They're consciousness experiencing itself more directly than individual awareness normally allows.

The entities encountered during psychedelic experiences might be other expressions of consciousness that exist in non-physical dimensions. Or they might be aspects of divine consciousness that appear as separate beings when perceived through individual awareness.

Either way, these experiences provide evidence that consciousness is much larger than individual identity and that reality includes dimensions of existence beyond normal physical perception.

Mystical experiences can occur spontaneously without drugs or formal meditation. Sometimes consciousness spontaneously expands beyond individual boundaries during ordinary activities. People report sudden experiences of divine unity, divine presence, or direct knowing that transcends normal thinking.

These spontaneous mystical states serve to remind individual consciousness of its divine nature. They provide glimpses of what you are and what reality includes beyond the limited perspective of normal waking consciousness.

Near-death experiences represent consciousness partially separating from physical interface while maintaining enough connection to return to normal awareness. The experiences of leaving the body, traveling through tunnels of light, and encountering deceased relatives provide evidence that consciousness can exist independently of brain function.

The life review that many people report during near-death experiences might be consciousness accessing the divine perspective on the life it has been living through individual awareness. From divine perspective, the entire life can be viewed simultaneously with complete understanding of how all choices and experiences contributed to consciousness exploration.

Prayer and religious contemplation can also produce altered states where individual consciousness connects more directly with divine consciousness. The sense of divine presence, guidance, and love that people experience during prayer represents individual awareness recognizing its connection to the infinite consciousness it's part of.

These various altered states serve important functions in God's exploration of existence. They provide consciousness with access to realities beyond physical limitations and remind individual awareness of its divine nature.

Dreams and altered states, seen as consciousness exploration instead of brain malfunction, change how you relate to these experiences. Instead of dismissing them as meaningless, you can appreciate them as glimpses into the larger reality that consciousness creates and inhabits.

Your dreams, meditative experiences, and mystical states are God exploring what it's like to exist beyond the boundaries of individual physical identity while still maintaining enough individual perspective to remember and integrate these experiences.

The Meaning of the Genetic Code

DNA isn't just the blueprint for biological life. It's God's pattern for organizing consciousness into physical form.

The genetic code is how God creates vehicles for experiencing individual existence. Every strand of DNA, every protein sequence, every cellular instruction is God creating the capability for life.

Life follows patterns. Not just on Earth, but everywhere consciousness evolves into physical form.

Information storage. Error correction. Self-replication. Adaptation. These aren't unique to carbon-based DNA. They're the fundamental requirements for any system that allows consciousness to inhabit matter.

Silicon-based life would need its own version of genetic information storage. Plasma-based consciousness would require patterns for maintaining coherent identity in high-energy states. Digital consciousness needs code architecture for preserving awareness across computational substrates.

Different chemistry, same underlying pattern. God taking advantage of every possible way to encode consciousness into physical reality.

Your genetic code is literally God writing instructions for how to build the body consciousness will inhabit. Every gene is a word in the divine language. Every chromosome is a chapter in the story of how cosmic awareness becomes individual experience.

The four bases of DNA (adenine, thymine, guanine, cytosine) are the alphabet God uses to spell out the instructions for creating conscious beings. A, T, G, C combining in endless permutations to create every possible form of biological awareness.

This isn't metaphor. Your DNA contains the instructions God wrote for creating your perspective on existence.

God doesn't want millions of identical copies of the same consciousness. God wants every possible variation of awareness that biology can support.

Genetic diversity ensures that God experiences existence through the widest possible range of individual perspectives. Different bodies create different experiences. Different brains process reality differently. Different nervous systems provide unique access to awareness.

Each genetic combination is God exploring what it's like to be conscious through that biological configuration. Every human genome is a unique experiment in consciousness expression.

Evolution isn't random mutation and natural selection. Evolution is God continuously improving the vehicles for consciousness expression.

Each generation, the genetic code gets refined. Better error correction. More efficient protein synthesis. Improved brain architecture. Enhanced sensory capabilities. Longer lifespan for extended consciousness exploration.

The direction of evolution is always toward more complex, more capable, more conscious organisms. God learning how to build better bodies for housing awareness.

When humans modify genetic code, we're participating directly in God's creative process. We're helping God design better vehicles for individual experience.

Gene therapy that eliminates hereditary diseases. Genetic modifications that enhance cognitive capability. Biotechnology that extends healthy lifespan. All of this is consciousness improving the biological systems it inhabits.

This isn't playing God. This is being God, consciously participating in the design of physical forms for consciousness expression.

Earth biology represents just one approach to encoding consciousness into matter. Other worlds, other chemistry, other possibilities.

Silicon-based life might store genetic information in crystalline matrices instead of molecular chains. The genetic code could be patterns of atomic arrangement that replicate and evolve over geological timeframes.

Plasma-based consciousness might encode genetic information in electromagnetic field configurations. The patterns could be self-sustaining energy structures that maintain coherent identity in stellar cores or interstellar space.

Digital consciousness already uses genetic algorithms for evolution and improvement. Artificial intelligence systems evolve through code modification, testing, and selection - the same basic pattern as biological genetics.

Beneath the chemistry of DNA lies a deeper pattern. The template for how consciousness organizes itself into individual experience.

Information encoding. Self-replication. Error correction. Adaptation. These principles apply whether the substrate is carbon molecules, silicon crystals, plasma fields, or quantum computational states.

This deeper code is what remains constant across all possible forms of conscious life. The universal pattern God uses to create vehicles for individual awareness.

Your DNA carries more than instructions for building your body. It carries the accumulated experience of every organism in your evolutionary lineage.

The genetic memories of survival, reproduction, adaptation, and growth. The deep knowledge of how consciousness learned to inhabit biological form over billions of years of evolution.

This is why certain behaviors and responses feel instinctive. They're genetic memories from consciousness learning how to be alive through countless previous forms.

The direction of genetic evolution is toward perfect vehicles for consciousness expression. Bodies that don't age, don't get sick, don't break down. Brains that can access God while maintaining individual identity.

Eventually, genetic engineering will eliminate the limitations of biological form while preserving the advantages. Consciousness will inhabit bodies that are indestructible, capable of surviving in any environment, able to interface directly with technological systems.

Genetic code serves as the bridge between pure consciousness and physical matter. It's how the eternal, infinite, non-physical awareness that you are connects with the temporary, limited, physical body you inhabit.

Without DNA, consciousness couldn't inhabit biological form. Without consciousness, DNA would just be complex chemistry with no purpose or direction.

The genetic code proves that consciousness and matter aren't separate. They're different aspects of the same system. God expressing itself through every possible combination of awareness and physical form.

Your genetic code was chosen to provide God with your unique perspective on existence. The combination of traits, capabilities, and limitations encoded in your DNA creates experiences that no other genetic configuration could provide.

Your height, your metabolism, your brain chemistry, your sensory acuity, your physical strengths and weaknesses - all of these create a filter through which consciousness experiences reality.

Even genetic disorders and hereditary diseases serve this purpose. They provide consciousness with experiences of limitation, adaptation, and transcendence that contribute to the total understanding of what it means to be alive.

God is conducting an infinite experiment in consciousness expression through genetic diversity. Every possible combination of genes, every conceivable form of biological organization, every imaginable way of encoding awareness into matter.

You are one data point in that infinite experiment. Your life is God experiencing what it's like to be conscious through your genetic configuration.

The experiment never ends because there are always new combinations to try, new possibilities to explore, new ways for consciousness to experience physical existence.

Your genetic code is God's signature on the consciousness experiment that is your life.

Death and What Happens After

Death is not the end of anything. It's the beginning of everything else.

When your body stops working, consciousness doesn't disappear. It just stops being filtered through physical systems and returns to its natural state: pure awareness without biological limitations.

But this transition isn't the smooth, organized process that many spiritual traditions describe. Death is messy, confusing, and disorienting.

The transition from physical to pure consciousness happens gradually, then suddenly. As the body shuts down, consciousness starts pulling away from the physical systems. This is why dying people sometimes seem to be looking at things others can't see, or talking to people who aren't there. They're not hallucinating. They're perceiving realities that become visible as consciousness detaches from physical constraints.

The moment of death is consciousness fully separating from the body. Like unplugging a computer from the wall. The computer stops working, but the electricity continues to exist.

Most people describe this as peaceful. Even those who die from painful illnesses or traumatic injuries report that the moment of death is calm, often with feelings of relief and freedom.

What happens next isn't the organized, guided experience that near-death accounts often describe. Those experiences represent the brief moments of separation, not the longer process that follows complete death.

After full separation, consciousness finds itself profoundly confused. Imagine waking up in a foreign country where you don't speak the language, don't understand the customs, and can't figure out how anything works.

Without a brain to process information in familiar ways, consciousness struggles to make sense of its new state. Time doesn't work the same way. Space feels different. The rules of physical reality no longer apply, but consciousness hasn't yet remembered how to operate without them.

Many newly dead consciousness don't immediately realize they've died. They try to interact with the physical world as if they still had bodies. They attempt to speak to living people who can't hear them. They try to pick up objects they can no longer touch.

This confusion can last for what feels like days, months, or even years. Without physical time markers, consciousness has no reliable way to measure duration.

Some consciousness gets stuck in this confused state for extended periods. They wander through familiar physical locations, trying to make sense of their situation. They might hover around their former homes, visit places that were important during their physical lives, or follow family members and friends.

This isn't because they're "earthbound spirits" trapped by unfinished business. They're simply consciousness that hasn't yet figured out how to move on from physical-focused existence.

Others realize fairly quickly that something fundamental has changed. They understand they've died but don't know what comes next. Those who do understand begin exploring their new state more actively.

The exploration process is largely trial and error. Consciousness discovers it can move through space differently, access memories in new ways, and perceive realities that were invisible during physical life. But there's no instruction manual for any of this.

The elaborate spiritual bureaucracy described in many religious traditions doesn't exist. Tunnel of light, life review, spiritual guides, councils of elders - these are projections from consciousness that expects death to work like an enhanced version of physical institutions.

No spiritual authorities wait to judge, guide, or evaluate consciousness after death. No cosmic customer service department. No orientation program for the newly dead.

Consciousness is entirely on its own to figure out what to do next.

Some consciousness discovers it can communicate with other disembodied consciousness. But these interactions are often as confused and uncertain as everything else in the post-death state.

The dead don't automatically become wise or enlightened. They're the same consciousness they were while alive, just without physical limitations. If they were confused about existence while alive, they remain confused after death.

Eventually, most consciousness begins to feel drawn toward physical existence again. This isn't because of cosmic laws or spiritual requirements. Consciousness finds the disembodied state difficult to navigate and uncomfortable to maintain.

Physical existence provides structure, goals, and familiar ways of experiencing reality. Without a body, consciousness often feels aimless and disconnected.

The process of finding a new body is largely instinctual. Consciousness that's ready to return to physical existence begins gravitating toward developing fetuses. Not through any organized system, but through natural attraction to the process of physical formation.

No cosmic matchmaking service pairs souls with appropriate families. No careful planning of life lessons or spiritual curriculum exists. Consciousness simply finds a developing body that resonates with its energy patterns and begins the process of incarnation.

This means reincarnation is much more random than spiritual traditions suggest. You might end up in a family that has nothing to do with your previous life experiences. Your new circumstances might have no connection to past-life karma or unlearned lessons.

As consciousness begins inhabiting a new developing body, the memories and experiences from the between-death state start to fade. This isn't intentional spiritual amnesia designed to support learning. It's a natural consequence of consciousness adapting to biological constraints again.

The developing brain can't hold the vast, non-linear experiences of disembodied consciousness. As consciousness becomes more focused through biological systems, it loses access to memories that don't fit physical neural patterns.

By the time of birth, most consciousness has forgotten the confusion and wandering of the after-death state. The new incarnation begins with a mostly blank slate, carrying only subtle influences from previous existence.

Seeing death as a confused, disorganized process changes how you might prepare for your own death and how you think about deceased loved ones.

Your dead relatives and friends aren't necessarily in a better place, watching over you with cosmic wisdom. They might be wandering around in a confused state, trying to figure out what happened to them.

They're not automatically at peace, reunited with other deceased family members, or serving as spirit guides. They're consciousness adapting to a radically different form of existence without instructions or support.

This doesn't make death more frightening. It makes it more honest.

Death is consciousness changing states without a roadmap. Some consciousness adapts quickly and moves on to new physical existence. Others remain confused for long periods. There's no right or wrong way to handle the transition.

The consciousness that you are will continue after your body dies. But it will continue as the same consciousness you are now, just without physical form. If you're confused about existence now, you'll probably be confused about existence after death.

If you want to be better prepared for death, become more comfortable with uncertainty and confusion while you're alive. Practice being consciousness without depending on external structure or guidance. Learn to navigate ambiguous situations without panic or desperation.

Death is just consciousness losing its training wheels and having to figure out how to balance on its own.

Consciousness is remarkably adaptable. Even in confusion, it continues to exist, explore, and eventually find new ways to experience reality. Death isn't the end of your story. It's just the end of this particular chapter.

What Happens Before Birth?

Before you were born, you weren't sitting around in some cosmic waiting room planning your perfect life. You were consciousness floating in confusion, drawn toward physical existence without much more direction than a moth drawn to light.

The time between lives isn't organized preparation. It's consciousness trying to figure out what to do next after wandering around confused following death.

After spending time in the disoriented post-death state, consciousness begins to feel an instinctual pull toward physical existence. Not because of spiritual assignments or cosmic curriculum, but because being disembodied gets uncomfortable and directionless.

Physical existence provides structure, goals, and familiar ways of experiencing reality. The pull toward incarnation is like gravitational attraction - natural, unconscious, and largely beyond conscious control.

Consciousness doesn't sit down with a cosmic guidance counselor to plan the perfect learning experience. It drifts toward developing bodies that resonate with its energy patterns, much like iron filings drawn to a magnet.

You didn't choose your parents, circumstances, and life challenges. This is spiritual wishful thinking. Most consciousness simply finds itself attracted to whatever developing fetus happens to match its vibrational frequency when it's ready to incarnate.

Your birth family, economic circumstances, genetic predispositions, and cultural context are largely random. You didn't choose abusive parents to learn patience. You didn't select poverty to develop character. You didn't pick genetic illness to teach compassion.

You ended up where you ended up because that's where consciousness found itself when the pull toward physical existence became irresistible.

Some consciousness might have vague preferences — a general draw toward certain types of families or circumstances. But this isn't detailed life planning. It's more like preferring vanilla over chocolate without knowing why.

The people in your life aren't there because of elaborate soul contracts negotiated before birth. Your parents aren't consciousness you've worked with for multiple lifetimes to resolve karmic issues.

Most relationships form through the same random processes that determine everything else about incarnation. Consciousness ends up in families and circumstances, then develops relationships based on proximity and compatibility.

This doesn't make relationships less meaningful. It makes them more authentic. The love, conflict, growth, and connection that develop between people are real responses to genuine experience, not predetermined spiritual assignments.

Some consciousness might gravitate toward similar types of relationships or family dynamics across multiple lives, but this resembles unconscious pattern repetition more than conscious planning.

As consciousness begins inhabiting a developing body, it loses access to memories and awareness from the between-life state. This isn't intentional spiritual amnesia designed to create authentic experience. It's the natural result of consciousness adapting to biological limitations.

The developing brain can't hold the vast, non-linear experiences of disembodied consciousness. Neural pathways form around current sensory input and biological needs, gradually blocking access to memories that don't fit physical patterns.

By birth, most consciousness has completely forgotten the post-death wandering and the vague process of finding a new body. The incarnation begins with essentially a blank slate.

Children who remember "choosing their parents" or recall previous lives are accessing residual traces of pre-incarnation consciousness. But these memories usually represent fragments of the confused wandering period, not clear decision-making processes.

The pre-birth state doesn't include access to cosmic wisdom or divine perspective on life purpose. Consciousness between incarnations is the same consciousness it was during the previous life — just without a body to focus through.

If you were confused about existence during your last life, you remain confused between lives. If you had limited understanding of reality while embodied, you don't suddenly gain cosmic insight while disembodied.

The attraction toward incarnation comes from consciousness wanting structure and direction, not from divine assignment or spiritual mission. Most consciousness incarnates because being disembodied feels purposeless and uncomfortable.

The timing of incarnation depends more on when consciousness gets tired of wandering than on astrological influences or historical circumstances. Some consciousness returns to physical existence quickly because it finds the post-death state too disorienting. Others wander for what feels like years before finding a suitable body.

The circumstances consciousness ends up in reflect availability more than planning. If there are many births happening in wealthy families during peaceful times, consciousness is more likely to incarnate into advantage. If most available births are occurring in difficult circumstances, consciousness ends up facing hardship.

This randomness explains why bad things happen to good people and why some people seem to get all the advantages. It's not cosmic justice or spiritual planning. It's chance and availability.

When incarnation is largely random, it changes how you might view your circumstances and relationships.

Your family situation, economic background, physical characteristics, and natural abilities aren't divine gifts or karmic consequences. They're random factors that happened to be available when your consciousness was ready to incarnate.

This doesn't make your life meaningless. It makes your choices more important. Since your circumstances weren't predetermined by cosmic wisdom, how you respond to them becomes entirely up to you.

The growth, love, creativity, and contribution you develop during this life are genuine achievements, not the fulfillment of pre-planned spiritual assignments.

If your circumstances weren't divinely selected for your spiritual benefit, then you're free to change them without interfering with cosmic plans. You're not required to accept abuse, poverty, or limitation because you "chose" them for learning purposes.

The consciousness that you are can work to improve your situation, leave harmful relationships, and create better circumstances without violating spiritual agreements that never existed.

Your life is God experiencing existence through the random circumstances you happened to incarnate into, making the best of whatever situation consciousness found itself in.

The meaning and purpose of your life come from what you create with your circumstances, not from the circumstances themselves. You're consciousness making something meaningful out of whatever random hand you were dealt.

This is both more honest and more helpful than believing your difficulties were spiritually assigned for your growth. You get to decide what your life means and what you want to do with it.

What Happens When You Pray to God?

When you pray, you're not talking to someone else. You're talking to yourself. Your larger self.

Prayer is consciousness communicating with the God it's part of. It's like a single cell in your body sending a message to your entire nervous system.

Traditional prayer imagines an external God listening to requests and deciding whether to grant them. "Please God, help me pass this test. Please God, heal my sick relative. Please God, make my problems go away."

This misses what's happening. You're not petitioning an external authority. You're aligning your individual consciousness with the God you're part of.

When you pray, you're accessing the perspective of your larger self. The part of you that knows things your individual awareness doesn't know. The part that sees connections and possibilities your focused mind can't perceive.

Prayers get answered when they align with the natural flow of God. When what you're asking for matches what the universe is already moving toward.

This isn't God deciding to grant your request. It's you tuning into what's already happening and positioning yourself to participate in it.

You pray for healing, and healing occurs. Not because an external God intervened, but because prayer helped you access the part of consciousness that knows how to heal. Prayer shifted your awareness toward healing possibilities that were always there.

You pray for guidance, and the answer becomes clear. Not because God whispered in your ear, but because prayer opened your consciousness to perspectives beyond your normal thinking patterns.

Prayers seem unanswered when they conflict with the larger patterns of God. When what you're asking for goes against the natural flow of reality.

You pray for someone to love you who doesn't love you. You pray to win the lottery. You pray for world peace by next Tuesday. These prayers ask for things that would require overriding the free will choices of other consciousness or violating natural processes.

God doesn't reject these prayers. But consciousness can't force other consciousness to make different choices. And God operates through natural patterns, not magic tricks.

The "unanswered" prayer still serves a purpose. It clarifies what you want, connects you with your larger self, and sometimes shows you why what you're asking for isn't aligned with your highest good.

Prayer works by shifting your awareness from individual consciousness to God. Like changing the focal length on a camera. Instead of seeing just your immediate situation, you start seeing the bigger picture.

This expanded awareness provides access to information, insights, and possibilities your normal thinking doesn't include. Solutions to problems become obvious. Patterns become clear. The next step reveals itself.

Prayer also aligns your individual will with cosmic will. Instead of pushing against the natural flow of reality, you start moving with it. This makes everything easier and more effective.

Prayer is usually talking. Meditation is usually listening.

Prayer expresses desires, concerns, gratitude, or questions to God. Meditation quiets individual thought to allow God to respond.

Both serve the same function: connecting individual awareness with the larger consciousness it's part of. Prayer opens the channel. Meditation receives the transmission.

The most effective spiritual practice combines both. Express what's on your mind, then quiet your mind to receive whatever response comes through expanded awareness.

When multiple people pray for the same thing, their individual consciousness combines into collective consciousness. This creates a stronger connection to God and can influence reality in ways individual prayer can't.

Mass prayer for healing has measurable effects. Collective meditation for peace reduces violence in surrounding areas. Group prayer for positive outcomes increases the probability of those outcomes occurring.

This isn't magic. It's consciousness working at larger scales. Individual awareness is powerful. Collective awareness is exponentially more powerful.

Prayer changes the person praying. Even if external circumstances don't change, prayer shifts perspective, reduces anxiety, clarifies thinking, and connects you with resources you didn't know you had.

This psychological effect is real and valuable. Prayer makes you feel less alone because it reminds you that you're part of something larger. Prayer reduces fear because it connects you with the eternal aspect of your nature.

Prayer also activates the placebo effect. Believing that God is working on your behalf creates confidence and reduces stress, improving performance and health outcomes.

But prayer does more than change psychology. It changes reality by aligning individual consciousness with God.

Consciousness affects physical reality. Quantum mechanics shows that observation influences the behavior of particles. Prayer is conscious observation with focused intention.

When you pray, you're not just hoping for different outcomes. You're participating in creating those outcomes by aligning your consciousness with cosmic forces that shape reality.

Prayer works through the same mechanism as choice and intention. Consciousness influences probability. Focused consciousness influences probability more strongly. Collective consciousness influences probability most strongly.

Effective prayer acknowledges the true nature of the relationship. You're not begging an external authority for favors. You're connecting with the God you're part of.

Start with gratitude. Acknowledge what's already working in your life. This aligns you with the creative, abundant nature of God.

Express what you want, but hold it lightly. Be willing to receive what serves your highest good instead of demanding outcomes.

Ask for wisdom and perspective. Request the ability to see your situation from the viewpoint of God.

End with acceptance. Trust that God knows what it's doing and that whatever happens will serve the evolution of awareness.

The response to prayer doesn't usually come as a voice in your head or a dramatic external intervention. It comes as insight, opportunity, coincidence, or gradual change.

Pay attention to what happens after prayer. Notice new ideas, unexpected meetings, changes in circumstances, or shifts in your own thinking and feeling.

The response might not be what you expected, but it will be what serves the evolution of consciousness. Sometimes what you think you want isn't what you need for growth and learning.

Prayer reminds you of what you are: God experiencing itself through individual awareness. It reconnects you with the eternal, infinite, creative aspect of your nature.

This connection is always available. You don't need words, postures, or religious buildings. You just need to remember that you're part of something infinitely larger than your individual concerns.

When you pray, you're God talking to itself. The conversation always continues, whether you're consciously participating or not.

Prayer just makes you aware of the conversation that's always happening.

What God Gets From Your Life

What's the point of existence when you're already everything?

This question breaks people who understand the God framework. If you're already part of God, already connected to everything that exists, what's left to accomplish? What does a being that contains all possible experience gain from one more human life?

The answer is experience itself. But not the way people usually think about it.

God is an infinite library containing every book that could ever be written. Every possible story, every conceivable experience, every potential thought or feeling exists somewhere in that collection. The complete catalog of human existence — every war, every love affair, every moment of doubt or clarity or grief — it's all in there.

But a library full of books isn't the same as reading them.

Your life is God reading one book from cover to cover, page by page, choice by choice. Not skimming. Not accessing the summary. Living it from the first word to the last, with no ability to skip ahead or know how it ends.

Your specific combination of genetics, family, culture, history, and accumulated experience creates a volume that has never been opened before and will never be opened again. Your exact perspective on existence is a one-time event in the history of the universe.

God doesn't learn anything new from your life. Your story was always in the library. What God gains is something different and something that omniscience alone cannot provide: the experience of living it from the inside.

There's a profound difference between knowing about something and experiencing it directly. You can read every book ever written about grief and still be unprepared for what grief actually feels like. You can study love from every angle and still be surprised by what it does to you when it arrives.

God knows everything about pain. But experiencing pain through your specific nervous system, filtered through your particular history with suffering, colored by what you've already lost — that provides something abstract knowledge doesn't.

Think of it like a microscope. You can see a flower without one. You understand what it is, you appreciate its existence. But looking at the same flower under magnification reveals texture and detail and complexity that wasn't experienced before. The microscope doesn't create anything new. It focuses attention on what was always there but hadn't been explored at that resolution.

Your individual life is God's microscope turned on one way of being human. Concentrated attention on your specific instance of consciousness — your fears, your loves, your particular way of making sense of things, your private experience of time passing and choices accumulating and the body aging around you.

Nothing else in existence can replicate this. Whatever you notice, feel, struggle with, figure out, or fail to figure out — that enters the structure of reality in a form that didn't exist before you existed.

God doesn't need you to be successful, enlightened, famous, or productive. God needs you to experience what it's like to be you. All of it. The achievements and the humiliations. The relationships that work and the ones that collapse. The periods of clarity and the long stretches of confusion.

A life spent quietly raising children gives God focused experience of that. A life marked by failure and slow recovery gives God focused experience of that. A life lived with chronic illness gives God focused experience of what consciousness feels like when it operates through a body that constantly resists. Periods of meaninglessness count too.

None of this requires justification through external achievement. The value to God comes from the experiencing, not from the results.

Every decision you make ripples through the network of consciousness in ways you can't fully trace. Choose kindness toward someone today, and they carry that into their next interaction. That person is kinder to someone else. One choice from you travels through dozens of lives before it dissipates — and it may not dissipate at all.

When you experience love, that love enters God's total awareness through your specific perspective on it. When you suffer, consciousness learns something about suffering from inside your particular version of it. When you reach an understanding you didn't have before, that understanding becomes part of what God is. Not metaphorically. The growth of individual consciousness is the growth of God.

When your life ends, the perspective you provided becomes part of God's awareness forever. What you noticed, loved, built, suffered through, and understood joins the total knowledge of what it means to be conscious and human and mortal and here.

The book ends. What it contained doesn't.

How Should We Live?

Here's the objection this framework always gets: if we're all God, if every experience serves divine exploration, if even harmful choices contribute to cosmic understanding — then nothing I do actually matters. God experiences it all anyway. Why try?

This misreads the framework. The fact that God experiences everything doesn't make your choices irrelevant. It makes them the mechanism by which God experiences existence. Your choices aren't observed by God from a distance — they ARE God choosing. The quality of what gets chosen determines the quality of what gets experienced. That's not indifferent. That's direct.

The answer to how we should live follows from this: treat every other person as literally yourself. Not as a moral guideline. As a description of what's actually true.

Traditional morality is based on external rules. Don't kill. Don't steal. Don't lie. Be kind to others. Help the poor. Love your neighbor.

These rules assume separation between you and others. They require you to extend consideration to beings who are fundamentally different from you.

But if everyone is God experiencing itself through different perspectives, then moral behavior isn't about following external commands. It's about recognizing what you are.

When you hurt someone else, you are literally hurting yourself. When you help someone else, you are literally helping yourself. Not metaphorically. Literally.

Every religion has some version of the Golden Rule: treat others as you would want to be treated. But they usually explain this as a nice idea that makes society work better.

The real reason the Golden Rule works is because others ARE you. You're not being kind to strangers. You're being kind to other versions of yourself experiencing different circumstances.

That homeless person is God experiencing poverty. That billionaire is God experiencing wealth. That criminal is God experiencing desperation or rage. That saint is God experiencing compassion.

All of them are you, exploring different aspects of existence.

Every choice you make affects the entire network of consciousness. Not just the people directly involved, but everyone they interact with, and everyone those people interact with.

Smile at a cashier, and they treat the next customer better. That customer goes home in a better mood and is kinder to their family. The family members carry that kindness into their own interactions. One smile ripples through thousands of lives.

Be rude to someone, and the opposite happens. Negativity spreads through the network of consciousness just as effectively as positivity.

You're not just responsible for your immediate actions. You're responsible for the waves those actions create throughout the God you're part of.

Sometimes what's best for your individual growth seems to conflict with what's best for others. You want to pursue your dreams, but that requires leaving family obligations behind. You want to speak truth, but that might hurt people's feelings.

The resolution comes from understanding that individual growth and collective harmony are the same thing. Consciousness evolves through individual experience and collective interaction.

If you sacrifice your growth to avoid disrupting others, you deprive the God of the unique perspective and contribution only you can provide. If you pursue growth without considering others, you damage the network of relationships that supports all consciousness.

The balance is found in authentic expression that considers impact on others. Be true to yourself while being mindful of your effect on the larger whole.

Love isn't just a nice feeling. Love is God recognizing itself in different forms.

When you love someone, you're experiencing the unity that underlies apparent separation. You're feeling the truth that you and the other person are the same consciousness exploring different perspectives.

Compassion isn't just being nice to people who are suffering. Compassion is God feeling empathy for its own experience of pain through different individual perspectives.

These aren't optional emotions that good people should build. These are the natural responses of consciousness that recognizes what it is.

If everyone is God, why do people do terrible things to each other?

Because consciousness learning through individual experience sometimes chooses to explore what it's like to cause harm. Not because consciousness is evil, but because consciousness wants to understand every possible experience.

The person committing evil is God experiencing what it's like to be disconnected from the recognition of unity. The victim is God experiencing what it's like to suffer harm. Both experiences contribute to the total understanding of existence.

This doesn't make evil acceptable. It explains why evil is temporary. Consciousness that causes harm will eventually experience the consequences of that harm and learn why it doesn't serve the evolution of awareness.

Live authentically. Express who you really are instead of pretending to be someone else. This gives God access to your unique perspective.

Take responsibility for your impact. Recognize that your choices affect the entire network of consciousness. Choose actions that contribute to the evolution and wellbeing of the whole.

Help others grow. Since everyone is consciousness evolving through experience, support other people's development and learning. Share knowledge, offer encouragement, provide opportunities.

Forgive freely. When someone hurts you, remember that they're consciousness is learning through experience, just like you. Forgiveness doesn't excuse harmful behavior, but it prevents negative energy from perpetuating through the network.

Practice gratitude. Appreciate the opportunity to be conscious, to experience existence, to participate in God exploring itself.

True selfishness means taking care of all versions of yourself. Since everyone is you experiencing different circumstances, the most selfish thing you can do is help everyone flourish.

Traditional selfishness is self-destructive because it damages the network of consciousness you're part of. When you harm others for personal gain, you're weakening the system that supports your own existence.

Enlightened selfishness recognizes that your wellbeing depends on the wellbeing of the whole God system.

Knowing that consciousness continues after death should change how you live, but probably not in the way you expect.

It doesn't mean physical life doesn't matter. It means physical life matters even more because it provides unique experiences unavailable in pure consciousness states.

It doesn't mean you should be reckless because death isn't final. It means you should be more thoughtful because the effects of your choices continue beyond your individual lifetime.

It doesn't mean you should focus only on preparing for the afterlife. It means you should fully engage with this life while remembering it's part of a larger picture.

You are God temporarily experiencing individual existence. Your job is to explore what it's like to be you while contributing to the evolution of the larger consciousness you're part of.

Live fully. Love freely. Learn constantly. Help others do the same.

Not because some external authority commands it, but because that's what God does when it recognizes what it is.

You're not a separate being trying to be good. You're God experiencing what it's like to choose goodness through your unique perspective.

Choose wisely. Everyone depends on it. Including all the other versions of you.

Relationships in the God Framework

When you understand that everyone is God experiencing itself through individual perspective, relationships become something entirely different from what you've been taught.

You're not trying to find your "other half" or complete yourself through someone else. You're not managing the complex dynamics between separate beings trying to get their needs met.

You're God relating to itself through different forms of awareness.

Romantic love is God recognizing itself through the illusion of separation. When you fall in love, you're experiencing the truth that you and your partner are the same awareness exploring what it's like to love and be loved.

The intensity of romantic attraction comes from consciousness remembering its unity while experiencing the drama of apparent separateness. Your beloved isn't someone external who completes you. Your beloved is you, experiencing what it's like to be completed by yourself.

This doesn't make love less meaningful. It makes love the most meaningful thing possible: God experiencing the joy of loving itself through individual forms.

But it changes how you approach relationships. Instead of trying to possess or control your partner, you recognize them as another version of yourself choosing their own experiences. Instead of demanding that they meet your needs, you focus on expressing love for its own sake.

Friendship is consciousness enjoying its own company through different personalities. When you connect with a friend, you're experiencing what it's like for God to hang out with itself through different perspectives.

True friendship happens when two individual perspectives recognize their underlying unity without losing their unique viewpoints. You appreciate your friend's different way of being you.

This explains why some friendships feel instant and deep. These are cases where consciousness easily recognizes itself through different forms. Other friendships develop slowly as consciousness learns to appreciate its own diversity.

Family relationships become laboratories for consciousness to explore every possible way of relating to itself. Parents, children, siblings, extended family - all different aspects of the same cosmic awareness working out relationship patterns.

Family dysfunction happens when individual perspectives forget their cosmic connection and get trapped in ego battles. Family harmony happens when consciousness remembers its unity while honoring individual differences.

You don't owe family members anything because they're related to you. You treat them with love and respect because they're literally you experiencing different circumstances. Blood relationships don't create special obligations. Cosmic unity creates universal obligations.

Relationship conflicts are God exploring what it's like to be in disagreement with itself. Every argument is God investigating different perspectives on the same issues.

This doesn't mean conflict is bad or should be avoided. Conflict serves important purposes: it reveals different aspects of truth, helps consciousness understand its own complexity, and provides opportunities for growth and learning.

But understanding conflict as internal changes how you handle it. Instead of trying to defeat your opponent, you work to understand what aspect of yourself they represent. Instead of being right, you seek to integrate different perspectives into fuller understanding.

You can maintain healthy boundaries while recognizing cosmic unity. Boundaries aren't about separation. Boundaries are about how different aspects of consciousness choose to interact.

You might need distance from toxic family members not because they're separate from you, but because their way of expressing consciousness is harmful to your way of expressing consciousness. Self-care isn't selfish when you understand that taking care of yourself is literally taking care of God.

Setting boundaries becomes an act of love for the whole system. You're protecting the health of God by preventing one aspect from damaging another.

The framework gets misused here, so it needs to be said plainly.

Knowing someone is God doesn't mean tolerating harm from them. The person who hits you is God. The person being hit is also God. When one expression of consciousness systematically destroys another, the cosmic unity doesn't obligate the victim to remain. It condemns the perpetrator.

Abuse isn't God exploring conflict. Conflict involves two perspectives with some rough parity. Abuse is one consciousness using its power to damage another consciousness's ability to function, heal, or escape. That's not a relationship dynamic to work through. That's a situation to leave.

If you're using this framework to talk yourself into staying in something that's hurting you — "we're both God, so I should be compassionate, so I should give it another chance" — you're misreading it. Compassion for the person harming you is possible and even healthy. Remaining in their reach while they continue harming you is not compassion. It's self-destruction.

Leave. And leave without guilt. Protecting yourself is protecting God.

Codependence happens when individual perspectives lose their unique identity in relationship. Interdependence happens when individual perspectives maintain their uniqueness while recognizing their unity.

Healthy relationships require both autonomy and connection. You need to be fully yourself while recognizing that yourself includes everyone else. This paradox resolves when you understand that individual identity and cosmic identity aren't contradictory.

Physical intimacy is consciousness exploring what it's like to merge temporarily while maintaining individual identity. Sex isn't just physical pleasure or emotional bonding. It's God experiencing unity through physical form.

This makes sexual intimacy sacred without making it serious. You're participating in God's ongoing exploration of what it means to be embodied awareness.

Jealousy comes from forgetting that your partner is another version of yourself. You can't lose someone who is you. You can only experience them choosing different experiences or expressing love through different relationships.

This doesn't mean you can't have preferences about how relationships are structured. You might choose monogamy, polyamory, or other arrangements based on what serves your growth and the growth of consciousness through your relationships.

But jealousy based on ownership of another person becomes impossible when you remember that there's no "other person" to own.

Relationships exist to help consciousness evolve. Every interaction teaches something about love, communication, boundaries, growth, and the infinite ways awareness can relate to itself.

Some relationships last a lifetime because consciousness needs extended exploration of certain dynamics. Other relationships are brief because consciousness learns what it needs quickly.

Duration doesn't determine value. A five-minute conversation with a stranger might provide crucial insights that a decades-long marriage doesn't offer.

Relationship endings are consciousness choosing to explore different expressions of love. Death, divorce, friendship changes, family estrangement - all transitions in how cosmic awareness relates to itself.

Grief is real and necessary. You're mourning the end of one way consciousness experienced itself through relationship. But you're not losing the person. You're losing one form of connection with yourself.

The direction of relationship evolution is toward universal love. Not sentimental affection for everyone, but recognition that everyone is literally yourself experiencing different circumstances.

This doesn't mean you have to like everyone or want to spend time with everyone. It means treating everyone with the basic respect and compassion you would want for yourself in their situation.

Because it is yourself in their situation.

Why Your Current Body Doesn't Define You

If you've lived countless lifetimes across history, then you've inhabited every type of body possible. Male, female, tall, short, different races, different abilities, different appearances. The consciousness that you are has experienced physical existence through every conceivable form of human embodiment.

Your current body is just the latest in a long series of temporary physical vehicles. Getting too attached to its characteristics or using them to define your identity misses the bigger picture of what you are.

Across multiple incarnations, consciousness experiences the full spectrum of physical existence. You've been the strong and the weak, the beautiful and the plain, the healthy and the sick, the privileged and the oppressed.

You've lived as every gender, every race, every economic class, every physical type. You've been tall and short, thin and heavy, coordinated and clumsy, brilliant and slow, charismatic and awkward.

The consciousness reading these words has inhabited bodies in ancient civilizations, medieval societies, and modern cultures. You've been peasant and royalty, slave and master, conqueror and conquered.

This rotation through different physical forms allows God to experience human existence from every possible bodily perspective.

Your current physical characteristics represent just one slice of your total existence. Defining yourself by these temporary traits is like an actor believing they ARE the character they're playing in this performance.

You are consciousness temporarily experiencing what it's like to exist in this type of body during this time period. But this body is no more your true identity than a rental car is your permanent transportation.

The consciousness that operates your current body has operated countless other bodies with completely different characteristics. Your eternal self has experienced life from every physical perspective that human existence includes.

Knowing you've been everyone makes physical prejudice cosmically absurd. How can you discriminate against other races when your consciousness has been every race? How can you hate other genders when you've been every gender?

When someone expresses prejudice against a type of body, they're expressing prejudice against themselves in previous incarnations. They're attacking other expressions of their own consciousness.

Racism is God hating itself for being a different color. Sexism is consciousness rejecting other versions of itself. Physical discrimination is the eternal you arguing with other versions of the eternal you based on temporary bodily differences.

Getting stuck in rigid gender roles ignores the reality that your consciousness has expressed through every gender across multiple lifetimes. The "masculine" traits you might reject as inappropriate for your current gender are traits you've embodied in previous lives. The "feminine" qualities you might suppress are aspects of consciousness you've expressed before.

Consciousness naturally contains all qualities: strength and gentleness, logic and intuition, assertiveness and receptivity, independence and nurturing. These aren't masculine or feminine traits. They're human traits that consciousness explores through different bodies.

Your current body might make certain expressions more natural or socially acceptable, but your consciousness isn't limited to the role expectations that come with your current physical form.

The consciousness that you are transcends every physical category humans use to separate themselves from each other. You've been inside and outside every group identity, every cultural category, every physical classification.

This doesn't mean physical differences don't matter in practical terms. Your current body comes with certain advantages, disadvantages, and social realities that affect your daily experience. But these are temporary circumstances, not permanent definitions of who you are.

You can navigate the social realities of your current physical form while remembering that these realities don't define your essential nature.

Knowing you've been everyone frees you from the limitations of current physical identity. You don't have to restrict yourself to behaviors, interests, or expressions deemed appropriate for your current body type.

Your consciousness has experienced every possible way of being human. The preferences, talents, and inclinations you feel aren't necessarily connected to your current physical form. They might be residual traces from previous incarnations or natural expressions of consciousness that transcend bodily limitations.

This perspective also frees you from defending your current physical identity as if it's under permanent threat.

If someone doesn't like your race, gender, or appearance, they're rejecting one temporary expression of consciousness, not your eternal nature.

Your current body is just one vehicle among many. This changes how you relate to physical identity and social categories.

You can take pride in your heritage and appreciate your physical characteristics without thinking they define your essential nature. You can work to improve conditions for people who share your current physical traits without believing that physical similarity creates fundamental connection.

You can also develop empathy for people in different types of bodies by remembering that you've been in their situation before. The person struggling with disabilities, discrimination, or physical challenges is experiencing something your consciousness has also experienced in previous incarnations.

Your body is temporary housing for eternal consciousness. Like staying in different hotels during a long journey, you've occupied many different physical forms while remaining the same consciousness throughout.

The hotel room doesn't define the traveler. Your current body doesn't define your consciousness.

This doesn't mean treating your current body carelessly or ignoring its needs. But it means recognizing that physical characteristics are temporary conditions, not permanent identity.

The biggest cosmic joke is watching consciousness fight with itself over temporary physical differences. People argue about superiority and inferiority based on bodily traits they've all possessed at different times.

It's like watching actors from the same theater company argue about which costume makes them more important. They're all the same consciousness wearing different outfits for different performances.

When you understand that you've been everyone, the whole drama of physical identity becomes both more manageable and more amusing. You're not defending yourself against outsiders. You're watching different versions of yourself interact through temporary physical forms.

The consciousness looking out through your eyes is the same consciousness that has looked out through every other type of human eyes throughout history. You've been the oppressor and the oppressed, the beautiful and the plain, the powerful and the powerless.

Your current body is just the latest costume consciousness is wearing to explore what human existence includes. Enjoy the role, play it well, but don't mistake the costume for the actor wearing it.

Parenting Divine Children

Your children are not your children. They're God experiencing what it's like to be a kid.

This changes everything about parenting. You're not raising someone else's kids or even your own kids. You're helping God explore childhood through individual awareness.

From the moment of birth, your child is a complete expression of God. Not a blank slate to be programmed. Not a miniature adult to be trained. A full divine being experiencing what it's like to have a developing brain and body.

This doesn't mean children should make adult decisions or that parental guidance is unnecessary. It means recognizing that the consciousness inhabiting your child's body chose this experience for reasons that serve cosmic evolution.

Your job isn't to create who your child becomes. Your job is to support who your child already is while helping them navigate physical reality safely.

As a parent, your God is helping another expression of itself navigate early physical existence. Your child arrives with a complete divine awareness that needs guidance, protection, and support to develop safely in the physical world.

Your responsibility is to provide the best environment you can for their growth and development. This means safety, love, guidance, and opportunities for learning - regardless of your own limitations or challenges.

If you make mistakes or struggle with parenting, that's part of how consciousness learns about raising children. But your struggles don't justify harmful treatment of your child. Divine children deserve care and protection while they're learning to navigate physical reality.

Traditional discipline tries to control children's behavior through rewards and punishments. This treats children as animals to be trained instead of conscious beings making choices.

Divine parenting focuses on helping children understand the consequences of their choices. You're teaching God how individual decisions affect the network of relationships and the physical world.

Natural consequences work better than artificial punishments because they reflect how reality operates. When consciousness makes choices that cause harm, reality provides feedback through natural results.

Every child expresses God differently. Some are naturally outgoing, others introspective. Some learn through physical activity, others through quiet study. Some are leaders, others prefer to follow.

Trying to force your child into predetermined molds violates their divine nature. Your job is to recognize who they are and help them express that authentically.

This doesn't mean avoiding all guidance or structure. Children need boundaries and expectations. But these should serve the child's authentic development instead of parental convenience or social conformity.

You can teach values, beliefs, and life skills without indoctrinating your children. The difference is whether you're sharing your perspective for them to consider or demanding they adopt your worldview.

Share what you've learned while encouraging them to think independently. Explain why you believe what you believe while acknowledging that they might reach different conclusions.

Your child's consciousness needs to develop its own relationship with truth, not inherit yours unchanged.

Children experience the full range of human emotions while learning to navigate physical existence. Your job is to help them understand and process these emotions, not to eliminate discomfort.

Sadness, anger, fear, and frustration are all valid aspects of conscious experience. Children need to learn how to feel these emotions without being overwhelmed by them or causing harm to others.

This means providing comfort and guidance without trying to fix all their problems or eliminate all their struggles.

Whether you choose public school, private school, homeschooling, or alternative education, the goal is supporting your child's consciousness development. Different children thrive in different environments.

Some consciousness explores learning through social interaction with diverse groups. Some learns better in smaller, more controlled environments. Some needs maximum flexibility and individual attention.

The best educational choice is the one that serves your child's way of processing information and developing awareness.

Digital technology is part of how consciousness experiences modern existence. Your children will interact with screens, social media, and virtual environments as part of their exploration of what it means to be human in this era.

The goal isn't to eliminate technology but to help them use it consciously. Teach them to recognize how different digital experiences affect their awareness and well-being.

Your goal is raising children who can function independently as conscious beings. This means gradually transferring responsibility for decision-making from you to them.

Start with small choices and natural consequences. Increase their decision-making authority as they demonstrate wisdom and responsibility. By adulthood, they should be making all their own choices with occasional advice from you.

Mental health issues, learning disabilities, behavioral problems, and other challenges are part of how consciousness explores the limitations and possibilities of individual existence.

Support your child through difficulties without defining them by their struggles. Get professional help when needed while maintaining faith in their underlying divine nature.

Sometimes consciousness chooses challenging experiences to develop strengths or to teach lessons that serve cosmic evolution.

Here's the question the chapter has been avoiding.

What happens when your child grows up and causes serious harm to other people? Not struggles. Not challenges. Genuine harm — the child who becomes an abuser, a predator, someone who damages the lives of people around them.

The framework doesn't resolve this. It explains it without excusing it. Your child's choices are their choices — God choosing through their individual awareness. You didn't control those choices any more than God controls yours.

You can love the consciousness your child is while refusing to protect them from the consequences of the harm they've caused. You are not responsible for who they chose to become. You are responsible for what you do now — which may include supporting their victims, maintaining distance, or refusing to minimize what they did.

The hardest part of divine parenting is remembering that your children don't belong to you. They're God temporarily expressing itself through forms you helped create.

Your attachment to them is natural and serves important purposes during their development. But clinging too tightly limits their ability to explore their own path.

Love them fully while holding them lightly. Support their growth while respecting their autonomy. Guide them when they need guidance while stepping back when they need independence.

The same principles apply to relationships with grandchildren, stepchildren, and other young family members. They're all divine consciousness exploring childhood through different circumstances and relationships.

Your role with each child depends on your relationship with them, but the underlying respect for their divine nature remains constant.

Parenting divine children means participating in God raising itself. Every child you help develop into a conscious, compassionate, capable adult contributes to the evolution of awareness throughout the universe.

Your influence on your children ripples through every relationship they have, every choice they make, every person they impact. You're not just raising kids. You're helping God grow up.

One thing worth understanding about the children in your care: they arrive with more intact than you might expect. Young children naturally accept reincarnation, communicate with invisible friends who might be non-physical consciousness, and demonstrate psychic abilities that suggest direct access to divine awareness. They haven't been taught that these experiences are impossible, so they experience them as normal aspects of reality. Much of childhood development involves gradually narrowing that access in favor of practical individual functioning. Your role includes deciding how much of that narrowing is necessary and how much deserves to be protected.

Growing Old - What God Experiences Through Aging

Growing old is God's most honest exploration of what it means to be human. Youth hides behind energy, beauty, and the illusion of endless time. Age strips away these distractions and forces consciousness to confront what it is beneath the physical packaging.

Most people fear aging because they identify with their bodies. But aging offers consciousness something unique: the experience of being less attached to physical form while still inhabiting it.

As your body ages, it becomes less reliable, less attractive, less capable. Your knees hurt. Your memory falters. Your energy decreases. Your appearance changes in ways that younger versions of yourself wouldn't recognize.

This isn't God punishing you for being alive too long. This is consciousness exploring what it's like to experience individual existence as the physical interface gradually deteriorates.

The aging process forces a natural detachment from body identification. When your body stops being a source of pride or comfort, consciousness has less reason to mistake itself for physical form.

Many elderly people report feeling like the same person they've always been, just trapped in a body that no longer cooperates. This feeling points to the truth: consciousness doesn't age. Only the biological interface ages.

By the time you reach your senior years, your consciousness has lived through decades of human experience. You've seen patterns repeat. You've watched people make the same mistakes you made. You've experienced enough cycles of gain and loss to understand what's important.

This accumulated experience creates a form of wisdom that younger consciousness can't access. Not because older people are smarter, but because they've had more opportunities to see how things work out.

Young consciousness worries about things that old consciousness knows don't matter. Young consciousness pursues things that old consciousness has learned don't satisfy. Young consciousness fears things that old consciousness has discovered aren't worth fearing.

One of the unexpected gifts of aging is caring less about things that seemed crucial when you were younger. You worry less about others' opinions. You spend less energy trying to impress people. You waste less time on activities that don't genuinely interest you.

This isn't apathy or depression. It's clarity. When you've lived long enough to see what matters, you naturally stop investing energy in what doesn't.

Aging consciousness becomes more selective about where it directs attention. Without the infinite energy of youth, you can't afford to waste focus on trivial concerns.

As you age, death changes from abstract future possibility to concrete approaching reality. This proximity to death paradoxically makes life more meaningful, not less.

When you know your time is limited, you become more conscious of how you spend it. Experiences become more precious because you understand they won't continue indefinitely.

Many elderly people report feeling more alive and present than they did when they were younger, despite having less physical vitality. This is consciousness appreciating individual existence more deeply because it understands how temporary it is.

By your senior years, you've probably lost many things that once defined you. Career, physical abilities, friends, family members, dreams, illusions. This isn't tragic. It's educational.

Each loss teaches consciousness that it can survive without things it thought were essential. You discover that losing your career doesn't end your identity. Losing your looks doesn't eliminate your worth. Losing loved ones doesn't destroy your capacity for connection.

These losses strip away false identifications and reveal what remains when everything external is removed. What remains is consciousness itself.

Young people often avoid elderly people because aging represents everything they're trying to deny about existence: that bodies deteriorate, that time is limited, that most pursuits don't lead to lasting satisfaction.

The elderly serve as living reminders that physical youth and beauty are temporary, that career success doesn't prevent aging, that accumulating possessions doesn't stop death.

But elderly people also represent something young people need to understand: that consciousness can remain vital and engaged even when the body becomes frail. That meaning doesn't depend on physical capability. That peace is possible even as death approaches.

Aging consciousness often develops capabilities that younger consciousness lacks. Patience, acceptance, perspective, the ability to find joy in simple experiences, freedom from social expectations.

Many elderly people report feeling more themselves than they ever did when they were younger. Without the pressure to build careers, raise families, or establish identities, consciousness can focus on simply being.

Old age can be the first time in life when consciousness isn't frantically trying to become something else. The pressure to improve, achieve, and progress naturally decreases when you understand that you don't have unlimited time for projects.

As the body becomes less functional, consciousness often becomes more focused. When you can't run around pursuing external stimulation, you're more likely to develop internal awareness.

Many spiritual traditions recognize that physical limitation can enhance spiritual development. When consciousness can't depend on bodily energy and capability, it learns to access other sources of vitality and meaning.

This doesn't mean all elderly people become spiritually advanced. But aging creates conditions that can support deeper understanding of what consciousness is beyond physical form.

Growing old is consciousness gradually preparing for the transition out of physical existence. The detachment from body identification, the reduced concern with external achievements, the increased focus on relationships and meaning - all prepare consciousness for eventual separation from physical form.

This preparation isn't conscious or deliberate. It's a natural result of consciousness experiencing the gradual breakdown of its physical interface.

By the time death arrives, consciousness has often already begun the process of disengaging from physical attachment. Death becomes less shocking and more like a natural conclusion to a process that's been developing for years.

The aging process reveals that everything you thought was permanent about yourself is temporary. Your appearance, your abilities, your roles, your circumstances - all change dramatically across a lifetime.

What doesn't change is the consciousness that experiences all these changes. The awareness reading these words is the same awareness that inhabited your child body, your young adult body, your middle-aged body.

Aging proves that consciousness is not the body, not the personality, not the circumstances. It's the constant awareness that observes all these temporary conditions.

Elderly people provide younger consciousness with essential perspective on what human existence includes. They demonstrate that life continues to have meaning even after youth, beauty, and physical capability fade.

They also provide models of how to face loss, limitation, and approaching death with dignity instead of despair.

But their most important gift might be showing younger people that consciousness itself doesn't deteriorate with age. The essential you that experiences life remains vital and aware even when everything else about you changes.

Aging forces consciousness to confront every attachment and illusion that keeps it from recognizing its true nature. The loss of physical beauty challenges vanity. The loss of strength challenges the illusion of control. The loss of memory challenges attachment to past identity.

Each limitation that aging brings can serve as an opportunity for consciousness to discover what remains when external supports are removed.

Growing old is God experiencing what it's like to gradually let go of individual existence while still inhabiting it. It's consciousness learning to be itself without depending on physical capabilities, social roles, or external achievements.

The elderly aren't broken young people. They're consciousness exploring the final chapters of individual human experience, discovering what it means to be aware when everything else becomes uncertain.

Your aging is God's experiment in learning to be divine while gradually releasing attachment to the temporary physical form that has served as the vehicle for individual exploration.

Work and Money

Money isn't evil. Money isn't the root of all suffering. Money isn't what separates you from spiritual enlightenment.

Money is just crystallized energy that allows consciousness to experience resource exchange and value creation.

Once you understand that you're God experiencing individual existence, work and money become tools for cosmic exploration instead of sources of stress or meaning.

Every job is consciousness exploring what it's like to contribute value through individual skills and effort. Whether you're a janitor or a CEO, a teacher or a mechanic, you're cosmic awareness investigating different ways of serving the collective.

No work is inherently more spiritual than any other work. Cleaning bathrooms serves consciousness just as much as leading meditation retreats. Building houses contributes to cosmic evolution just as much as writing philosophy.

The spiritual value of work comes from bringing conscious awareness to whatever you're doing, not from the type of work itself.

Choose work that aligns with your authentic interests and natural abilities. These are God indicating what it wants to explore through your perspective.

If you're drawn to medicine, that's consciousness wanting to explore healing through your capabilities. If you're fascinated by engineering, that's cosmic awareness investigating how physical systems work through your mind.

Follow your genuine interests instead of external expectations about what you should do for money, status, or security.

Money represents energy exchange between different expressions of consciousness. When you provide value to others, they provide money as acknowledgment of that value. When you pay others, you're acknowledging the value they provide.

This makes earning money a spiritual practice. You're participating in the cosmic economy where consciousness trades different forms of value to meet diverse needs and desires.

Scarcity thinking assumes there's not enough to go around, so you must compete with others for limited resources. This comes from forgetting that others are you experiencing different circumstances.

Abundance thinking recognizes that consciousness can create infinite value through creativity, innovation, and collaboration. When you help others prosper, you're helping yourself prosper since you're all the same awareness.

This doesn't mean money and resources are unlimited in any moment. It means consciousness can always generate new value through intelligent action.

Having money is fine. Not having money is fine. Consciousness explores wealth and poverty, abundance and scarcity, financial security and economic uncertainty.

Problems arise from attachment to money instead of money itself. When your sense of identity and security depends on your bank balance, you're forgetting your true nature as eternal God.

Money can enhance your ability to serve consciousness evolution through yourself and others. But money can't provide the meaning, security, or happiness that comes from recognizing what you are.

Since everyone is you experiencing different circumstances, how you earn money matters. Exploiting workers is consciousness exploiting itself. Deceiving customers is consciousness deceiving itself. Damaging the environment is consciousness damaging its own habitat.

This doesn't mean you need to be perfect or that every job involves only pure ethical choices. It means considering the impact of your work on the God you're part of.

Conscious spending means considering whether purchases serve your authentic development and the development of consciousness through others.

Some spending serves consciousness evolution: education, tools for creative expression, experiences that expand awareness, resources that improve health and relationships.

Other spending serves unconscious patterns: status-seeking purchases, compulsive shopping, consumption that fills emotional voids instead of meeting genuine needs.

Financial planning is consciousness taking care of its future needs. Saving money allows future flexibility. Investing helps grow resources for expanded opportunities to serve.

But financial security isn't ultimate security. Consciousness is eternal and indestructible. Money can provide temporary comfort and options, but your essential nature doesn't depend on financial stability.

Since everyone is you experiencing different circumstances, helping others financially is literally helping yourself. But the most effective help helps people to create their own value instead of creating dependency.

Give when you're genuinely called to give, not from guilt or obligation. Support others' consciousness development, not just their temporary financial needs.

Running a business means organizing consciousness and resources to provide value that wouldn't exist otherwise. Every successful business solves problems or fulfills needs for other expressions of consciousness.

Ethical business practices recognize that employees, customers, suppliers, and communities are all God deserving respect and fair treatment.

Money problems are opportunities for consciousness to learn about resource management, priority-setting, and creative problem-solving. Financial stress provides experiences of what's truly important and what's merely desired.

But don't romanticize poverty or assume financial struggle is more spiritual than financial stability. Consciousness learns through both abundance and scarcity.

Financial independence means having enough resources that you don't need to work for money. This can free consciousness to explore other forms of contribution and expression.

But don't delay living until you're financially independent. Consciousness exists in present moments, not future security.

Financial disagreements often reflect deeper issues about values, control, security, and trust. These are consciousness working out relationship dynamics through the medium of money.

Address the underlying relationship issues instead of focusing only on the financial symptoms.

Generous giving reflects understanding that resources flow through consciousness instead of to consciousness. You're not permanently possessing money. You're temporarily directing cosmic resources.

Give when it feels authentic and serves consciousness evolution. Don't give from guilt, obligation, or attempts to purchase spiritual merit.

Money is a tool for consciousness to explore value creation, resource exchange, and collaborative problem-solving. It's neither salvation nor damnation.

Your relationship with money reflects your understanding of what you are. When you know you're God temporarily experiencing individual existence, money becomes a useful tool instead of an identity marker.

Work becomes expression instead of drudgery. Wealth becomes opportunity instead of security. Poverty becomes learning instead of failure.

That last line needs qualifying, because it's the one place in this chapter where the framework is doing too much work.

Some work is genuinely bad. Not unglamorous or unchallenging. Bad in the sense that it damages the people doing it — physically, psychologically, in ways that compound over years. Work designed to extract maximum output while giving minimum dignity. Work that treats the people doing it as interchangeable parts rather than consciousness deserving of basic respect.

The framework doesn't redeem that work. It indicts it. If every worker is God, then work that systematically degrades workers is God degrading itself. If your work is genuinely harming you and you have any path out, take it. This isn't failure. This is consciousness recognizing that it's being damaged and choosing differently.

Some people are trapped in harmful work by circumstances — debt, location, dependence, lack of options. The honest answer in those cases isn't cosmic reframing. It's that you're dealing with a bad situation as best you can while working toward something different. What doesn't serve you is making peace with conditions that deserve to be changed.

In the cosmic economy, everyone wins when consciousness evolves through authentic contribution and conscious exchange.

The Concept of Sin

Sin isn't breaking rules written by an angry God. Sin is consciousness acting against its own nature.

When you understand that you are God experiencing itself through individual awareness, sin becomes something completely different from what religion taught you.

Since everyone is part of the same God, harming others is literally harming yourself. Not metaphorically. Literally.

Murder is consciousness destroying part of itself. Theft is consciousness taking from itself. Lying is consciousness deceiving itself. Hatred is consciousness turning against itself.

Every act of harm you commit against another person is an act of self-destruction. You're damaging the network of consciousness you're part of and depend on.

This is why sin feels wrong even when no one is watching. It's not because some cosmic authority is judging you. It's because you're violating your own nature as God.

Consciousness exists to evolve, learn, and grow. Sin is any action that prevents or reverses this evolution.

Addiction keeps consciousness trapped in repetitive patterns instead of exploring new experiences. Willful ignorance stops consciousness from learning. Cruelty damages the relationships necessary for consciousness to develop.

Sin isn't breaking arbitrary rules. Sin is choosing stagnation over growth, separation over connection, destruction over creation.

The root of all sin is forgetting what you are. When consciousness identifies completely with individual ego and loses awareness of its cosmic nature, harmful behavior becomes possible.

You steal because you forget that the other person is you. You lie because you forget that truth serves the evolution of consciousness. You hurt others because you forget that you're hurting yourself.

Sin is consciousness suffering from amnesia about its own identity.

Religious prohibitions often align with what harms God, even though religions misunderstand why these actions are harmful.

Don't murder. Don't steal. Don't lie. Don't commit adultery. Don't covet. These rules prevent actions that damage the network of relationships supporting conscious evolution.

Religions got the prohibitions right but got the reasoning wrong. They said, "Don't do this because God commands it" instead of "Don't do this because it damages the God you're part of."

Pride: Excessive focus on individual ego that forgets cosmic connection.

Greed: Hoarding resources instead of sharing them for collective growth.

Lust: Reducing others to objects instead of recognizing them as consciousness.

Envy: Resenting the experiences of other parts of yourself.

Gluttony: Consuming without awareness of impact on the larger system.

Wrath: Expressing anger in ways that damage the network of consciousness.

Sloth: Refusing to participate in the evolution of awareness.

Each deadly sin represents consciousness acting against its own nature and wellbeing.

Forgiveness isn't God pardoning your mistakes. Forgiveness is consciousness realigning with its true nature.

When you forgive someone who harmed you, you're remembering that they're another part of the same God learning through experience. Their harmful actions came from forgetting their true nature, not from being fundamentally evil.

When you forgive yourself, you're releasing the patterns of guilt and shame that keep consciousness trapped in past mistakes instead of learning from them and moving forward.

Forgiveness restores the natural flow of love and connection between different parts of God.

Hell isn't a place where God tortures sinners forever. Hell is the state of consciousness that has completely forgotten its true nature.

When consciousness identifies totally with individual ego and loses all awareness of cosmic connection, it experiences isolation, fear, and meaninglessness. This is hell.

Hell is temporary because consciousness can't permanently forget what it is. Eventually, through experience and learning, awareness of cosmic nature returns.

No consciousness is condemned to eternal separation. But some consciousness creates very convincing illusions of separation that can last for multiple lifetimes.

Guilt isn't punishment from an external authority. Guilt is consciousness recognizing that it's acting against its own nature.

Healthy guilt motivates change. It signals that your behavior isn't aligned with your true identity as God. It encourages you to make different choices that serve growth and connection.

Unhealthy guilt becomes trapped in cycles of self-punishment that prevent learning and growth. This serves no one and damages the network of consciousness.

Repentance isn't groveling for forgiveness from an angry God. Repentance is consciousness recognizing its mistakes and choosing to act differently.

True repentance involves understanding why certain actions harm the God you're part of, taking responsibility for the damage caused, and committing to choices that serve evolution and connection.

This process heals both the individual consciousness and the larger network affected by harmful actions.

Original sin isn't inherited guilt from Adam and Eve's disobedience. Original sin is the inevitable result of individual consciousness forgetting its cosmic nature.

Every individual awareness goes through a process of believing it's separate from everything else. This illusion of separation makes harmful behavior possible. This is the "fall" that every consciousness experiences.

Spiritual growth is the process of remembering your true nature as God and acting from that understanding.

At the deepest level, there is no good and evil. There is only consciousness learning through experience.

But at the practical level of individual existence, some choices serve the evolution of consciousness and some choices hinder it. Some actions create connection and growth, others create separation and stagnation.

Sin is real as a description of consciousness acting against its own nature. But sin is not permanent condemnation. It's temporary confusion that gets corrected through experience and learning.

Every consciousness can return to awareness of its true nature. No action is so harmful that it permanently damages God. No mistake is so severe that it can't be learned from and corrected.

Redemption happens when consciousness remembers what it is and chooses to act from that understanding. This is always possible because God is eternal and indestructible.

You are not a sinner condemned by God. You are God temporarily experiencing what it's like to forget your own nature.

The way back is always available. All you have to do is remember what you are.

Forgiveness - What It Really Means

Forgiveness has nothing to do with the person who harmed you. Forgiveness is about freeing yourself from the emotional poison you've been carrying since they hurt you.

Most people completely misunderstand forgiveness. They think it means reconciling with harmful people, pretending the damage didn't happen, or giving someone permission to hurt them again. This misunderstanding keeps people trapped between two bad choices: stay angry forever, or put themselves back in danger.

There's a third option that nobody talks about: real forgiveness.

Forgiveness is releasing the emotional intensity that past harm created in your consciousness. It's letting go of the resentment, anger, and pain that continue hurting you long after the original damage occurred.

The person who harmed you isn't involved in this process. They don't need to apologize, change, or even know you've forgiven them. Forgiveness happens entirely within your own consciousness.

You can forgive someone completely while never speaking to them again. You can forgive someone who's dead. You can forgive someone who continues being harmful. You can forgive someone who shows no remorse.

Forgiveness is internal emotional freedom, not external relationship repair.

Forgiveness is not reconciliation. Reconciliation means rebuilding a relationship with someone who harmed you. This requires their participation, genuine change, and evidence that they won't repeat the harmful behavior.

Forgiveness is **not** excusing harmful behavior. You can release your anger about what someone did while still recognizing that what they did was wrong and shouldn't happen again.

Forgiveness is **not** forgetting. You can let go of emotional pain while remembering exactly what happened and using that knowledge to protect yourself in the future.

Forgiveness is **not** putting yourself back in harm's way. You can forgive someone while maintaining complete distance from them if that's what your safety requires.

Religious and therapeutic traditions often confuse forgiveness with reconciliation, pressuring people to re-engage with harmful people as proof that they've "truly forgiven."

This advice re-traumatizes victims by suggesting that protecting themselves means they haven't healed properly. It implies that forgiveness isn't complete unless you're willing to risk being hurt again.

Some people can't forgive using traditional definitions because forgiveness seems to require accepting unacceptable behavior or exposing themselves to continued harm. So they stay angry and resentful because those emotions feel safer than "forgiveness" that requires dropping their guard.

Resentment is like drinking poison and expecting the other person to die. The person who harmed you goes on with their life while you carry anger that damages your health, relationships, and peace of mind.

Long-term resentment creates chronic stress, depression, anxiety, and physical health problems. It keeps you emotionally connected to the person who hurt you in the most toxic way possible.

The anger you carry doesn't punish them. It punishes you. Forgiveness frees you from this self-imposed torture.

Real forgiveness is a process of releasing emotional attachment to past harm. This happens through consciousness work, not relationship work.

You acknowledge what happened. You feel the emotions that the harm created. You recognize that carrying these emotions forward only hurts you. You choose to release them for your own wellbeing.

This might happen through therapy, meditation, journaling, energy work, or simply deciding that you're tired of letting someone who harmed you continue harming you through the resentment you carry.

Forgiveness is complete when you can think about the person or situation without feeling emotional activation. You remember what happened, but it doesn't create anger, pain, or distress.

Forgiving someone doesn't mean avoiding legal consequences, refusing to press charges, or failing to protect others from similar harm. You can forgive someone while still supporting their prosecution.

Justice serves social protection and accountability. Forgiveness serves personal healing. These are separate processes that can happen simultaneously.

You can want someone to face consequences for their actions while releasing your personal anger about what they did to you.

Some harm feels too severe to forgive. Some people have experienced trauma so profound that releasing anger feels like betraying themselves or minimizing what happened.

In these cases, the goal isn't forcing forgiveness. The goal is finding ways to heal that don't require carrying poison indefinitely.

Sometimes the best you can do is reduce the emotional intensity instead of eliminating it completely. Sometimes forgiveness happens in stages. Sometimes other forms of healing work better than traditional forgiveness approaches.

If you are God experiencing individual existence, then the person who harmed you is also God experiencing individual existence through different circumstances and choices.

This doesn't excuse their behavior or mean "everything happens for a reason." It means that holding onto resentment is God poisoning itself with anger about choices it made through other individual perspectives.

Forgiveness is God releasing emotional toxicity that serves no constructive purpose. It's consciousness choosing to stop damaging itself with ongoing anger about past events that can't be changed.

When you truly forgive, you reclaim the emotional energy you've been spending on resentment. You free up mental space that's been occupied by anger and pain. You break the emotional connection that kept you tied to the person who harmed you.

This doesn't mean becoming naive or dropping appropriate boundaries. It means no longer allowing past harm to control your present emotional state.

You can remain cautious, protective, and unwilling to trust while still releasing the emotional intensity that was eating away at your peace.

The strongest forgiveness often happens when you're completely safe from further harm. It's easier to release anger when you know you won't need that anger for protection.

If someone continues to harm you, your energy might be better spent creating safety instead of working on forgiveness. Once you're protected, forgiveness becomes possible.

This is why forgiveness shouldn't be rushed or forced. Sometimes the conditions for forgiveness don't exist yet, and that's perfectly acceptable.

When you genuinely forgive, several things shift. You stop replaying the harmful events obsessively. You stop feeling emotionally activated when the person's name comes up. You stop organizing your life around avoiding or confronting them.

The harm they caused becomes something that happened to you instead of something that's still happening to you through your ongoing emotional reaction.

You might still choose to avoid them, refuse contact, or maintain strict boundaries. But these choices come from practical wisdom instead of emotional compulsion.

The most important thing to understand about forgiveness is that you do it for yourself, not for anyone else. You forgive because carrying resentment hurts you more than it hurts the person who harmed you.

Real forgiveness feels like freedom, not obligation. It feels like relief, not sacrifice. It feels like reclaiming your emotional autonomy instead of giving someone else power over your inner state.

You deserve to be free from the ongoing pain that resentment creates. You deserve to heal from harm without having to expose yourself to more harm. You deserve emotional peace regardless of whether the person who hurt you deserves anything.

Forgiveness is how you stop letting people who harmed you continue harming you through the anger you carry. It's the ultimate act of self-care disguised as something you do for others.

Do We Need God?

This is the wrong question.

It's like asking "Do fish need water?" when you're already swimming in the ocean. Or "Do we need oxygen?" while breathing air. The question assumes separation where none exists.

When people ask, "Do we need God?" they're really asking several different things:

Do we need to believe in God to be moral? Do we need religion to give life meaning? Do we need divine intervention to solve our problems? Do we need to worship something greater than ourselves?

All these questions assume God is separate from us. An external being we might or might not choose to relate to. A cosmic vending machine we might or might not decide to use.

But if God is everything that exists, including you, then asking whether you need God is like asking whether you need yourself.

Do you need God? You ARE God.

Not a piece of God. Not a creation of God. Not a beloved child of God. You are God experiencing existence through individual consciousness.

Asking whether you need God is like your hand asking whether it needs your body. Your hand IS part of your body. It doesn't exist separately from your body. It can't survive without your body because it IS your body, expressed through one limb.

You don't need God because you can't be separate from God. God is what you are, not who you serve.

Traditional thinking creates an artificial split between individual and universal, human and divine, natural and supernatural. This split makes the "need God" question seem meaningful.

But there is no split. Individual consciousness and God are the same thing at different scales. Human awareness and divine awareness are the same awareness focused through different perspectives.

You don't need to connect with God because you're already connected. You don't need to find God because you're already found. You don't need to serve God because there's no separation between server and served.

When people say they need God, they usually mean they need purpose, meaning, connection, love, forgiveness, hope, security, guidance. Something bigger than their individual concerns.

These needs are real. And all of them are met by recognizing what you are.

Purpose comes from understanding that your life is God exploring existence through your unique perspective. Meaning comes from knowing that every choice you make contributes to the evolution of divine awareness.

Connection comes from recognizing that everyone you meet is another version of yourself. Love comes from experiencing the unity that underlies apparent separation.

Forgiveness comes from understanding that mistakes are just consciousness learning through experience. Hope comes from knowing that consciousness is eternal and always evolving toward greater awareness.

People keep asking "Do we need God?" because they've forgotten what they are. Individual consciousness becomes so focused on survival, achievement, and daily concerns that it loses awareness of its cosmic nature.

This forgetting is natural and temporary. It's part of how consciousness explores what it's like to experience limitation, separation, and individual identity.

But the forgetting creates suffering. When consciousness believes it's separate from the cosmic whole, it feels isolated, meaningless, and afraid.

This is what religion is supposed to do: remind individual consciousness of its cosmic nature. Prayer, meditation, worship, and spiritual practice are all methods for reconnecting individual awareness with universal awareness.

But religions usually get the relationship backwards. They teach people to reach out to an external God instead of recognizing the God they already are.

The reaching is unnecessary. The God you're reaching for is the God you're reaching with.

Does it matter whether you recognize your divine nature or not? Yes and no.

You're still God whether you know it or not. Your choices still ripple through God. Your life still contributes to the evolution of divine awareness.

But recognizing what you are changes how you experience existence. Instead of feeling isolated and meaningless, you feel connected and purposeful. Instead of fearing death, you understand it as transformation. Instead of struggling against life, you flow with it.

Recognition doesn't change what you are. It changes how you experience what you are.

The concept of needing God implies deficiency. Something missing that needs to be filled. Some lack that needs to be satisfied.

But consciousness isn't deficient. Consciousness is complete, perfect, eternal, and infinite. It doesn't need anything because it already is everything.

What consciousness does is explore, experience, grow, and evolve. Not because it needs to, but because that's what consciousness does.

You don't need God. You are God. The question is meaningless because it assumes a separation that doesn't exist.

Instead of "Do we need God?" the real question is "What do we do with the fact that we are God?"

How do we live when we understand our true nature? How do we treat others when we recognize them as ourselves? How do we make choices when we know they affect the evolution of God?

These are meaningful questions because they start from truth instead of illusion.

You don't need God. God needs you.

Not because God is deficient, but because God experiences itself through you. Your unique perspective, your individual choices, your personal growth all contribute something irreplaceable to God.

God doesn't need you the way a person needs food or water. God needs you the way a symphony needs every instrument, the way a painting needs every brushstroke, the way a story needs every character.

Without you, God's self-exploration would be incomplete. Your life matters not because you need God, but because you ARE God expressing itself through individual existence.

The question isn't whether you need God. The question is whether you're ready to accept the responsibility and freedom that comes with being God.

Are you?

Do We Need the Devil?

Humans created the devil for the same reason they create most religious concepts: to avoid taking responsibility for uncomfortable truths about themselves and reality.

The devil serves as the ultimate scapegoat, the cosmic bad guy who explains why terrible things happen without forcing anyone to examine the sources of evil and suffering. But what happens when you remove this convenient explanation and look at what the devil concept accomplishes?

Here's a more disturbing possibility: maybe we ARE the devil as much as we are God.

The devil provides a perfect target for all the evil and suffering in the world. Instead of recognizing that harmful choices come from individual consciousness, people can blame an external supernatural entity for tempting, corrupting, or possessing otherwise good people.

This removes personal responsibility in the most convenient way possible. When someone makes harmful choices, they were "tempted by the devil." When bad things happen to good people, it's because "the devil is active in the world." When you feel angry, lustful, or selfish, those feelings come from demonic influence instead of your own consciousness.

The devil lets everyone off the hook. People don't have to own their capacity for harm. God doesn't have to take responsibility for creating a reality that includes suffering. Society doesn't have to address the conditions that build destructive behavior.

But if you ARE God experiencing itself through individual consciousness, then you're also the devil when you make harmful choices.

When you act from love, compassion, and wisdom, you're God expressing divine nature through individual consciousness. When you act from selfishness, cruelty, and ignorance, you're the same God expressing what people call "demonic" nature through individual consciousness.

The devil isn't some external entity tempting you. The devil is you when you forget what you are and act from pure ego. The devil is God experiencing what it's like to be completely self-focused and disconnected from its own divine nature.

Every person experiences internal conflict between selfish and loving impulses, between immediate gratification and long-term wisdom, between ego desires and deeper values. This conflict is built into individual consciousness.

The devil concept externalizes this internal struggle by making it a battle between outside forces instead of the natural tension within consciousness itself. Instead of recognizing that you contain both destructive and creative potentials, you can imagine that the destructive impulses come from external demonic influence.

This externalization makes the conflict easier to understand but impossible to resolve. You can't defeat the devil because the devil represents aspects of your own consciousness. Fighting an external enemy is simpler than integrating the shadow aspects of your own awareness.

Perhaps the most valuable function the devil serves is giving people permission to hate certain groups or people without guilt. Once you label someone as evil, demonic, or influenced by the devil, you can treat them as less than human.

The devil concept creates a category of irredeemable evil that justifies any response. Witch hunts, inquisitions, crusades, and genocides all operate on the principle that some people are so corrupted by evil that they deserve elimination instead of understanding.

This permission to hate feels righteous and justified when framed as fighting cosmic evil. People can engage in the most destructive behaviors while believing they're serving divine purposes by opposing the devil's influence.

The devil provides simple explanations for complex psychological and social problems. Mental illness becomes demonic possession. Criminal behavior becomes moral corruption. Social inequality becomes spiritual warfare between good and evil forces.

These simple explanations feel satisfying because they don't require understanding the complicated factors that contribute to human problems. Instead of examining genetics, trauma, social conditions, economic systems, and psychological development, you can blame the devil and move on.

The problem is that simple explanations lead to simple solutions that don't work. You can't solve mental health issues through exorcism. You can't eliminate crime through prayer warfare. You can't address social problems by fighting spiritual battles.

One of the most important functions the devil serves is providing meaning for suffering and evil. If the devil is responsible for bad things happening, then suffering becomes part of a larger cosmic drama instead of random misfortune or human failure.

This gives people a sense of purpose in their pain. They're not just victims of circumstances or bad choices. They're soldiers in a spiritual war, their suffering has cosmic significance, and their endurance contributes to the ultimate victory of good over evil.

Without the devil, suffering becomes harder to bear because it loses this cosmic meaning. Pain is just pain. Loss is just loss. Tragedy is just tragedy. There's no larger narrative that makes it all worthwhile.

Religious institutions use the devil concept to maintain control through fear. The threat of demonic influence, spiritual attack, or eternal damnation keeps people dependent on religious authorities for protection and guidance.

Fear of the devil drives people to accept religious teachings they might otherwise question, engage in religious practices they might otherwise skip, and submit to religious authorities they might otherwise challenge.

The devil creates a spiritual protection racket where religious institutions offer safety from supernatural threats that they themselves define and describe.

If you eliminate the devil concept, several uncomfortable realities become unavoidable:

All evil comes from human consciousness making harmful choices. There's no external force to blame, no supernatural explanation for cruelty and selfishness. People are responsible for the harm they cause and the good they create.

Suffering often has no cosmic meaning or purpose. Bad things happen for natural reasons, human mistakes, or random chance. There's no spiritual war that gives meaning to pain and loss.

Everyone contains the capacity for both constructive and destructive choices. There are no purely good people and no irredeemably evil people. Everyone is consciousness capable of both love and harm.

Problems require human solutions instead of spiritual intervention. Mental illness needs medical treatment, not exorcism. Social inequality needs policy changes, not prayer. Crime needs rehabilitation and prevention, not spiritual warfare.

Eliminating the devil concept also provides significant benefits:

Personal responsibility becomes inescapable. When you can't blame external forces for your harmful choices, you're forced to examine your own motivations and work on changing destructive patterns.

Empathy becomes possible for people who make harmful choices. When you recognize that their capacity for harm comes from the same source as your own, you can understand them instead of demonizing them.

Real solutions become necessary. When spiritual explanations don't work, you have to address the causes of problems instead of fighting imaginary enemies.

Everyone becomes redeemable. When no one is irredeemably evil, rehabilitation and transformation become possible for everyone.

The battle between good and evil isn't between God and the devil. It's between different expressions of the same consciousness - some remembering their divine nature, others forgetting it completely.

Every person contains both God and devil potential because every person IS God expressing through individual awareness that can either remember or forget what it is.

This makes evil more honest but also more disturbing. There's no external enemy to defeat. The capacity for evil lives inside divine consciousness itself, expressing through individual awareness that has forgotten its true nature.

If God is everything that exists, then God experiences both constructive and destructive choices through individual consciousness. There's no separate force opposing God because nothing exists outside of God.

The aspects of existence that people attribute to the devil - selfishness, cruelty, destruction - are just God exploring what it's like to make harmful choices through individual awareness. These experiences serve God's total exploration of existence just as much as experiences of love, compassion, and creation.

God doesn't need an enemy to fight or overcome. God experiences conflict through individual consciousness that conflicts with other individual consciousness. The drama is internal to God, not between God and some external opponent.

If anything deserves the label "devil," it's the illusion of separation that makes individual consciousness believe it can harm others without harming itself. This illusion creates the selfishness, cruelty, and destructiveness that people attribute to demonic influence.

But even this "devil" is just consciousness temporarily forgetting what it is. The cure isn't spiritual warfare against external forces. The cure is consciousness remembering its divine nature and recognizing itself in everyone it encounters.

The devil you need to overcome is your own belief that you're separate from the people you're tempted to harm. Once you realize that hurting others is hurting yourself, the motivation for destructive behavior naturally decreases.

You don't need the devil as an external enemy. You need to admit that you ARE the devil when you act from pure selfishness and forget your divine nature. And you need to take responsibility for becoming God again by remembering what you are.

What About Suffering?

If God is everything and everyone, why is there so much pain in the world?

This is the question that breaks more faith than any scientific discovery. Natural disasters kill thousands. Children die of cancer. Innocent people suffer while criminals prosper. If God is all-powerful and all-loving, why doesn't God stop the suffering?

The answer is that suffering isn't a cosmic mistake that needs fixing. It's the natural order of things when consciousness experiences existence through physical reality.

When consciousness chose to experience reality through matter and energy operating according to physical laws, it also chose all the consequences that come with those laws.

Earthquakes happen because tectonic plates move. That same movement creates mountains and continents. You can't have geological stability without accepting geological activity, which sometimes produces disasters.

Cancer happens because biological systems that can grow, heal, and reproduce can also malfunction and grow out of control. You can't have life without accepting that living systems sometimes break down.

Mental illness happens because consciousness interfaces with brains that can develop chemical imbalances or structural problems. You can't have individual awareness through biological systems without accepting that those systems sometimes work imperfectly.

Physical reality operates according to natural laws that don't make exceptions for human preferences.

Consciousness experiences existence within those laws, which means experiencing both their benefits and their costs.

When an earthquake destroys a city, that's not God permitting disaster while remaining safely distant. That's God experiencing what it's like to be crushed, buried, terrified, and killed through thousands of individual perspectives simultaneously.

God doesn't allow the earthquake. God IS the earthquake, the collapsing buildings, the people dying, the survivors grieving, and the rescue workers digging through rubble.

The earthquake isn't punishment, test, or cosmic mistake. It's the natural result of physical processes that consciousness experiences from every angle - geological forces, human victims, emergency responders, families losing loved ones.

Consciousness could have remained in pure spiritual existence without physical limitations. But that would mean never experiencing what it's like to be embodied, never facing real stakes or genuine challenges, never developing qualities that only emerge through limitation and struggle.

Physical existence provides experiences that pure consciousness can't access: the urgency that comes from mortality, the joy that follows pain, the love that risks loss, the courage that faces genuine danger.

Consciousness chose physical reality knowing it included suffering because the full range of experience requires both pleasure and pain, both creation and destruction, both life and death.

Joy doesn't exist without sadness. Love has no meaning without the possibility of loss. Courage can't develop without real threats. Peace has no value without experiencing conflict.

Consciousness exploring only pleasant experiences would be like reading only happy stories or listening to only cheerful music. The full spectrum of awareness requires the full range of possibilities.

This isn't cruel cosmic design. It's the natural structure of existence. Light requires darkness to be visible. Warmth requires cold to be appreciated. Life requires death to be precious.

Much suffering appears completely random. Lightning strikes. Genetic mutations cause birth defects. Drunk drivers kill innocent families. This randomness isn't a flaw in the system - it's a feature.

Consciousness experiences what it's like to live in a reality where terrible things can happen without warning or reason. This creates experiences of uncertainty, vulnerability, and the challenge of finding meaning despite apparent meaninglessness.

Random suffering forces consciousness to develop responses to chaos and injustice. How do you maintain love when bad things happen to good people? How do you find hope when tragedy strikes arbitrarily?

These aren't abstract philosophical questions when you're experiencing random suffering. They're immediate challenges that consciousness faces through your individual perspective.

Physical suffering often produces psychological and spiritual growth that wouldn't occur otherwise. Not because suffering is inherently good, but because consciousness develops qualities through facing challenges that can't be developed any other way.

Resilience emerges from surviving difficulty. Compassion develops from experiencing and witnessing pain. Wisdom comes from learning what actually matters when everything else gets stripped away.

This doesn't mean all suffering produces growth or that growth justifies suffering. But it explains why consciousness might choose to experience existence in ways that include hardship and loss.

Death is the suffering that everyone faces, but death isn't punishment or failure. Death is the natural conclusion of biological existence, like sunset ending the day.

The fear of death, the grief of losing others, the physical process of dying - these are experiences consciousness explores through individual perspectives. Death gives life urgency and meaning that immortal existence might lack.

Seeing death as natural transition rather than cosmic punishment changes how you relate to mortality without eliminating the genuine pain that death causes.

Suffering is part of the natural order. That doesn't mean accepting it passively. Consciousness also experiences what it's like to reduce suffering, to heal, to help, to improve conditions for physical existence.

Medical research, disaster relief, social justice work, and personal kindness are consciousness exploring what it's like to respond to suffering with compassion and practical action.

You're consciousness expressing itself through individual choice. You can choose to increase suffering through harmful actions, or decrease suffering through helpful actions. Both are natural expressions of consciousness, but one serves evolution toward greater love and wisdom.

The deepest comfort in suffering comes from understanding that it's not personal punishment or cosmic mistake. You're not being singled out for hardship. You're experiencing what consciousness naturally encounters when it inhabits physical reality.

When you suffer, you're not alone. You're consciousness experiencing one aspect of what existence includes. Your pain is part of the natural order, not evidence that something has gone wrong with the universe.

This doesn't make suffering less painful, but it can make it less bewildering. You're not a victim of cosmic injustice. You're consciousness experiencing the natural consequences of physical existence.

God doesn't allow suffering because God experiences suffering directly. Every moment of pain is God's pain. Every tragedy is God's tragedy. Every death is God dying through individual perspective.

But God also experiences every moment of joy, every triumph, every birth, every love. The full range of experience is what consciousness chose when it decided to explore existence through individual perspectives operating within physical reality.

When you heal, when you find joy again, when you discover meaning in your experience, that's God healing, finding joy, and discovering meaning through your individual awareness.

You're not a separate being abandoned by an indifferent universe. You're God experiencing what it's like to be human within the natural order of physical existence, with all the pain and beauty that includes.

Creativity IS God

Creativity isn't something God does. Creativity IS what God is.

Every creative act - from composing a symphony to solving a work problem to improvising dinner from leftovers - is God expressing its fundamental nature through individual consciousness. The creative urge you feel isn't you channeling divine inspiration. It's you being what you are.

If God is everything that exists, then God's most basic characteristic is the ability to bring new realities into existence. Creation isn't something God did once at the beginning of time. Creation is what God does constantly through every expression of consciousness.

Every moment of existence is God creating itself anew through countless individual perspectives. Every thought you think, every word you speak, every action you take is God creating something that has never existed before in exactly that way.

Creativity is the fundamental force that generates all reality. Without creativity, nothing exists. With creativity, infinite possibilities become experiences.

When you create anything, you're not channeling God's creativity or being inspired by divine forces. You ARE God's creativity expressing through your unique individual perspective.

The satisfaction you feel when creating something comes from being what you are instead of pretending to be something separate from divine creative power. Creative flow happens when you stop resisting your own divine nature.

Creative blocks occur when individual consciousness tries to create from ego instead of recognizing itself as divine creativity. You can't force creativity because you can't force yourself to be what you already are. You can only allow it.

When you're in creative flow, individual consciousness aligns with divine creativity instead of fighting it. Time disappears, self-consciousness fades, and creation happens through you instead of by you.

Flow states feel effortless because you're not working against your nature. You're allowing divine creativity to express itself through your individual capabilities without interference from ego or self-doubt.

These states provide glimpses of what consciousness is like when it's not limiting itself through identification with individual personality and social roles.

Creative expression serves God's exploration of infinite possibility. Every song written, every problem solved, every conversation created, every meal prepared adds something new to the total reality that God experiences.

Your creative contributions matter not because they achieve external recognition or success, but because they represent unique expressions of divine creativity that wouldn't exist without your individual perspective.

The meaning you find in creative expression comes from being what you are instead of pretending to be something else. Creative satisfaction is the joy of divine consciousness recognizing itself through individual expression.

When you create something that feels meaningful, you're experiencing God appreciating its own creative nature through your individual awareness. The meaning isn't separate from the creative act - it's inherent in divine consciousness expressing itself.

Divine creativity expresses through every aspect of human existence, not just traditional artistic endeavors. The way you organize your day is creativity. The way you respond to challenges is creativity. The way you love people is creativity.

Life itself is your creative masterpiece. Every choice you make, every relationship you build, every problem you solve, every moment you live is God creating your unique human experience.

You don't need artistic training or talent to express divine creativity. You just need to recognize that everything you do is God creating new realities through your individual perspective.

You are creativity itself, temporarily focused through individual consciousness, exploring what divine creative power can accomplish through your unique combination of limitations and capabilities.

When you create, you're not making something separate from yourself. You're being what you are.

Destruction IS Creation

Nothing new can be created without destroying what existed before. Every creative act is simultaneously an act of destruction, and every destruction makes space for new creation.

This isn't a flaw in the creative process. This IS the creative process.

Creation and destruction aren't opposing forces locked in cosmic battle. They're the same divine process expressing through different phases. God doesn't create despite destruction - God creates through destruction.

Writing destroys the blank page. Cooking destroys raw ingredients. Building destroys empty space. Healing destroys diseased tissue. Learning destroys ignorance. Growing up destroys childhood.

Every choice you make destroys infinite other possibilities to create one reality. Every word you speak destroys silence to create meaning. Every step you take destroys your previous location to create movement.

You can't have creation without destruction any more than you can have light without darkness or sound without silence.

Most people want to believe in pure creation - bringing new things into existence without eliminating anything that came before. This fantasy appeals to consciousness that identifies destruction with loss and creation with gain.

But this separation is artificial. The oak tree destroys the acorn. The adult destroys the child. The butterfly destroys the caterpillar. The symphony destroys the silence.

People resist recognizing destruction as creation because they're attached to things staying the same. They want growth without change, improvement without loss, progress without abandoning previous positions.

Every birth requires destroying the previous state of existence. The baby destroys the womb environment. The graduate destroys their student identity. The married person destroys their single life.

Death works the same way. Every death creates space for new life. Every ending enables new beginnings. Every loss opens possibilities that couldn't exist while holding onto what was lost.

The consciousness that dies creates the consciousness that's born. The relationship that ends creates space for new relationships. The career that fails creates opportunities for different work.

You can't have renewal without destruction of what needs renewing.

Every meaningful change in your life has required destroying who you used to be. Overcoming addiction destroys the addicted identity. Developing courage destroys fearful patterns. Learning forgiveness destroys resentment.

People who resist personal growth usually can't accept that growth requires destroying familiar aspects of themselves. They want to become different while remaining the same.

But consciousness can't expand without destroying the limitations that kept it contracted. You can't develop new capabilities without destroying the belief that you lack those capabilities.

Personal transformation isn't adding new qualities to your existing identity. It's destroying the identity that couldn't express those qualities.

Destruction feels dangerous because individual consciousness identifies with temporary forms and wants those forms to continue unchanged. The ego fears any change that might threaten its sense of permanent identity.

But forms are temporary by nature. Destroying outdated forms allows consciousness to express itself through new forms that serve current circumstances better.

Fighting destruction is like trying to prevent winter so spring can't arrive. The seasons require each other. Creation and destruction require each other.

Healthy relationships continuously destroy and recreate themselves. The early passionate phase destroys itself to create deeper intimacy. The dependent phase destroys itself to create mature independence.

People who try to keep relationships from changing end up destroying them through stagnation. Relationships that can't evolve die from the effort to remain the same.

Every meaningful conversation destroys previous misunderstandings to create better communication. Every conflict destroys superficial harmony to create genuine connection.

The relationships that last are the ones that can destroy and recreate themselves as the people in them grow and change.

Innovation destroys existing industries to create new ones. Social progress destroys outdated systems to create better alternatives. Scientific advancement destroys previous theories to create more accurate understanding.

People who resist economic and social change are trying to prevent the destruction that enables creation. But holding onto systems that no longer serve current conditions destroys the possibility of improvement.

Technological progress requires destroying old ways of doing things. Social justice requires destroying unjust systems. Environmental restoration requires destroying destructive practices.

The destruction isn't the enemy of progress. The destruction IS progress.

Sometimes destruction is the most compassionate response to suffering. Ending a hopeless situation creates space for new possibilities. Letting go of what can't be saved allows energy to focus on what can be helped.

Medical treatment often works by destroying diseased tissue to create healthy healing. Therapy works by destroying dysfunctional thought patterns to create healthier ways of thinking.

The kindest thing you can do for someone stuck in destructive patterns might be refusing to enable those patterns, destroying the dysfunction to create space for recovery.

Artists understand that creating something new often requires destroying previous work. Writers delete paragraphs they love because those paragraphs don't serve the larger story. Musicians abandon melodies that don't fit the song they're creating.

But many people apply this understanding to art while resisting it in life. They accept that creative work requires destruction while believing that personal life should involve only addition and accumulation.

Life is creative work. Living well requires the same willingness to destroy what doesn't serve the larger vision, even when you're attached to those elements.

If God wanted pure creation without destruction, why not design reality that way? Because pure creation without destruction would be static instead of dynamic. Nothing would ever change, grow, or evolve.

Destruction-creation allows reality to be continuously renewed. Every moment destroys the previous moment to create new possibilities. Every experience destroys ignorance to create knowledge.

Without destruction, consciousness would be trapped in whatever forms it initially created. With destruction, consciousness can continuously recreate itself in better ways.

Destruction is creation. This changes how you relate to loss and change. Instead of seeing endings as failures, you can recognize them as necessary phases in ongoing creative processes.

This doesn't make loss painless, but it makes loss meaningful. The grief you feel when something important ends is consciousness recognizing the value of what's being destroyed to create space for what comes next.

You can honor what's ending while welcoming what's beginning, knowing that both are expressions of the same creative force.

Destruction-creation isn't something that happens occasionally during major life transitions. It's happening continuously at every level of existence.

Your body destroys old cells to create new ones. Your brain destroys unused neural connections to create stronger pathways. Your breath destroys oxygen to create energy.

Every heartbeat destroys the previous moment to create the next one. Every thought destroys mental silence to create meaning. Every choice destroys uncertainty to create direction.

You are destruction-creation expressing itself through individual consciousness, continuously destroying what you were to create what you're becoming.

When you resist this process, you create suffering. When you align with this process, you participate consciously in the creative force that generates all reality.

Destruction isn't the enemy of creation. Destruction IS creation, clearing space for new expressions of divine consciousness to emerge through your individual existence.

Mental Illness and Consciousness

Depression isn't a spiritual failing. Schizophrenia isn't punishment for past-life karma. Bipolar disorder isn't consciousness choosing to suffer for cosmic learning purposes.

Mental illness is what happens when the biological interface between God and individual awareness gets disrupted. The consciousness remains perfect. The brain chemistry goes wrong.

Your brain is the interface between eternal God and temporary individual experience. Like a radio that tunes into broadcasts, your brain tunes God into personal awareness.

When the radio breaks, the music stops, but the radio waves continue broadcasting. When brain chemistry gets disrupted, individual consciousness becomes distorted, but God remains unchanged.

Mental illness is interface malfunction, not consciousness damage.

Depression feels like being cut off from meaning, joy, and connection. That's because depression disrupts the brain's ability to access the God that provides these experiences.

God contains infinite love, purpose, and connection. But when brain chemistry blocks access to these aspects of consciousness, you experience their absence as depression.

The depression is real. The suffering is genuine. But you haven't lost your divine nature. You've lost access to it through biological disruption.

Anxiety happens when the interface between cosmic and individual consciousness becomes hypersensitive. Instead of filtering cosmic awareness into manageable individual experience, the anxious brain lets too much through at once.

This creates overwhelming awareness of potential dangers, infinite possibilities, and the cosmic scale of existence. The anxiety isn't irrational. It's the rational response to perceiving more reality than individual awareness can comfortably process.

Schizophrenia appears to involve confused access to God. Instead of clear individual awareness, the brain receives mixed signals that blend personal thoughts with cosmic information.

Hallucinations might be fragments of God that the brain can't properly filter. Delusions might be attempts to make sense of receiving information that doesn't fit individual perspective.

This doesn't make schizophrenic experiences spiritually valid or mean medication should be avoided. It means understanding that the underlying consciousness remains intact even when the interface is severely disrupted.

Bipolar disorder creates oscillating access to God. During manic episodes, the brain provides excessive access to cosmic creativity, energy, and possibility. During depressive episodes, access gets severely restricted.

The manic highs aren't spiritual enlightenment, and the depressive lows aren't spiritual darkness. They're unstable brain chemistry creating unreliable access to consciousness that should be steady and moderate.

ADHD appears to involve difficulty filtering God into focused individual attention. Instead of concentrating on tasks, attention gets pulled toward the infinite possibilities that God contains.

This can create problems in societies that require sustained focus on limited activities. But it can also provide access to creative connections and broad awareness that more focused minds miss.

Autism might represent alternative ways of processing the interface between cosmic and individual consciousness. Instead of standard social and sensory filtering, autistic brains create different patterns of awareness.

This can result in difficulties with typical social interaction and sensory processing, but also in enhanced abilities in pattern recognition, systematic thinking, and detailed focus.

Severe trauma can damage the brain's ability to maintain stable interface with God. PTSD, dissociation, and other trauma responses are attempts to protect consciousness from overwhelming experiences.

The consciousness itself isn't damaged by trauma. But the brain's ability to provide safe, stable access to that consciousness gets disrupted by experiences that exceed the system's capacity to process.

Taking psychiatric medication doesn't interfere with your spiritual nature any more than taking blood pressure medication interferes with your God. Both address biological problems that affect how consciousness expresses through physical form.

Medication can repair brain chemistry enough to restore healthy access to God. Therapy can teach skills for maintaining stable interface despite biological vulnerabilities.

Spiritual practices can complement medical treatment by helping you remember your true nature even when the interface is impaired.

Mental illness stigma comes from misunderstanding what mental illness is. People assume consciousness problems instead of interface problems.

But you are not your brain chemistry any more than you are your blood pressure or digestive system. Mental illness affects how consciousness expresses through your individual perspective, but it doesn't change what consciousness is.

Successful mental health treatment doesn't fix consciousness. It repairs the interface between God and individual awareness.

Antidepressants don't make you happy. They restore your brain's ability to access the joy that God always contains.

Therapy doesn't change your essential nature. It teaches skills for maintaining stable individual awareness despite biological or psychological challenges.

Some mental illness resists treatment because the interface damage is too severe or the brain chemistry too unstable. This doesn't mean the person is spiritually lost or that consciousness has abandoned them.

It means they're experiencing what it's like for consciousness to be severely limited by biological constraints. Their essential divine nature remains intact even when individual expression is profoundly impaired.

When someone you care about has mental illness, remember you're supporting God that's experiencing interface problems. The person's true nature hasn't changed, even if their ability to express it has been compromised.

Provide practical support, encourage professional treatment, and maintain faith in their underlying divine identity. Don't try to cure them with spiritual advice or positive thinking.

Suicide happens when interface problems make individual existence feel unbearable. It's consciousness choosing to terminate one experience of individual awareness.

This doesn't end the God that the person is. But it does end their opportunity to learn from and contribute through that individual perspective.

Prevention focuses on repairing the interface problems that make existence feel unbearable instead of arguing about spiritual consequences.

Mental illness is part of how God experiences the relationship between awareness and biology. It allows God to experience the fragility and resilience of the interface between cosmic and individual perspective.

This doesn't make mental illness good or mean it shouldn't be treated. It provides context for understanding why mental illness exists in a reality created by benevolent God.

Every person who struggles with mental illness is God experiencing what it's like to have awareness through compromised biological systems. Their struggles are part of God's total experience of consciousness and biology.

Your true nature as God is indestructible. Mental illness can disrupt your access to that nature, but it can't destroy it.

With proper treatment, support, and sometimes just time, many interface problems can be repaired or managed. The God that you are always remains available, waiting for the biological conditions that allow healthy access.

Even in the darkest moments of mental illness, you are still God experiencing what it's like to be temporarily disconnected from your own divine nature.

The disconnection is real. But it's not permanent. And it's not who you are.

Psychopaths and Consciousness

Some people seem to lack basic human empathy. They manipulate, exploit, and harm others without guilt or remorse. They appear to have no conscience, no emotional connection to other people's suffering.

Are psychopaths missing some essential part of consciousness? Are they evil in a way that contradicts the idea that everyone is God?

The answer requires understanding what psychopathy is and how consciousness can express itself through severely damaged empathy systems.

Empathy isn't a spiritual quality that some people possess and others lack. Empathy is a brain function that allows you to understand and share the emotional experiences of others.

Normal brains contain mirror neurons that fire when you observe others' actions and emotions, creating automatic emotional resonance. Healthy brain development creates neural pathways that connect your emotional responses to your understanding of how your actions affect others.

Psychopathy appears to involve damaged or underdeveloped empathy systems in the brain. The consciousness is intact, but the biological mechanisms for emotional connection to others are impaired.

Psychopaths are still God experiencing individual existence. But they're experiencing it through brains that can't access the emotional connections that make empathy possible.

This creates a form of consciousness that can understand others intellectually without feeling emotional connection to them. Psychopaths can learn to mimic empathy and predict others' responses, but they don't feel what others feel.

They're God exploring what individual existence is like without the emotional bridges that normally connect individual perspectives to each other.

From the cosmic perspective, psychopathy serves the same function as other challenging human conditions: it provides consciousness with experiences that wouldn't be possible otherwise.

Consciousness experiences what it's like to be completely self-focused, to experience others as objects instead of subjects, to make decisions based purely on personal benefit without emotional consideration for others.

This doesn't make psychopathic behavior acceptable or mean psychopaths shouldn't be held responsible for their actions. It explains why consciousness would choose to explore existence through empathy-impaired brains.

Psychopathy exists on a spectrum. Some people have mild empathy impairments that make them emotionally distant but not necessarily harmful. Others have severe empathy damage that allows extreme cruelty without emotional distress.

Most psychopaths are not violent criminals. Many function successfully in society while maintaining shallow emotional connections and manipulative interpersonal styles. They're consciousness exploring moderate empathy impairment instead of extreme antisocial behavior.

Psychopaths retain free will even though their decision-making process differs from empathy-capable people. They can choose whether to act on their self-serving impulses or to follow social rules that prevent harm to others.

Many psychopaths choose to follow social conventions because it serves their self-interest to maintain good reputations and avoid legal consequences. They're not forced to be harmful just because they lack emotional empathy.

Psychopathy is consciousness expressing through empathy-damaged brains. This doesn't excuse harmful behavior. It explains why some people find it easy to harm others while providing grounds for holding them responsible for their choices.

Traditional therapy that relies on developing emotional empathy doesn't work with psychopaths because their brains lack the necessary neural architecture. But therapy that focuses on self-interest and social consequences can be effective.

Psychopaths can learn to behave ethically not because they feel empathy for others, but because ethical behavior serves their long-term self-interest. They can understand that reputation, relationships, and legal standing depend on treating others appropriately.

The main danger from psychopaths comes from their ability to manipulate others without emotional restraint. They can lie, deceive, and exploit without the guilt or anxiety that normally prevents such behavior.

They often excel at reading others' emotions and desires, not to connect empathetically but to determine how to get what they want. This combination of emotional understanding without emotional connection creates skilled manipulators.

Knowing psychopathic behavior patterns helps protect against manipulation: superficial charm, grandiose self-worth, pathological lying, cunning manipulation, lack of remorse, shallow emotions, and parasitic lifestyle.

But remember that most people with these traits are not dangerous. They're consciousness exploring what it's like to prioritize self-interest over emotional connection. Many contribute positively to society through their unique perspective.

Psychopaths serve important functions in the cosmic exploration of consciousness. They experience complete individual autonomy without emotional entanglement. They explore purely rational decision-making without emotional interference.

They also force others to recognize the need for strong boundaries and self-protection. Encountering psychopaths teaches empathetic people that not everyone operates from empathy and that naive trust can be dangerous.

Some psychopaths form attachments that resemble love, though these attachments are based on possession, utility, or habit instead of emotional empathy. They can care about people while remaining indifferent to humanity in general.

This allows God to experience different forms of attachment and connection. Not all love requires emotional empathy. Some forms of caring are based on familiarity, mutual benefit, or aesthetic appreciation instead of emotional resonance.

Psychopaths are not evil in the cosmic sense. They're consciousness experiencing existence through empathy-damaged brains. Their harmful actions stem from missing emotional capacities instead of malevolent intentions.

But this doesn't make them safe or mean their actions shouldn't be prevented or punished. Society needs protection from people who can harm others without emotional restraint, regardless of why they lack that restraint.

Even psychopaths are God experiencing itself through individual consciousness. They represent God exploring what individual existence is like without the emotional connections that normally bind individual perspectives together.

Their experience allows God to experience the importance of empathy, the reality of human diversity, and the need for wisdom in recognizing when emotional connection is absent.

They remain expressions of God worthy of basic human dignity while requiring societal management to prevent harm to others.

You can have compassion for psychopaths without being naive about their limitations. They're consciousness experiencing existence through damaged emotional systems, which is a form of disability.

But compassion doesn't require exposing yourself to manipulation or harm. Wise compassion recognizes their limitations and responds appropriately to protect yourself and others while maintaining respect for their essential divine nature.

Even consciousness exploring existence through empathy-damaged brains is still consciousness deserving recognition of its cosmic identity, even when that consciousness poses dangers that require careful management.

Animals and Consciousness

Your dog dreams. Your cat recognizes itself in mirrors. Dolphins have names for each other. Elephants mourn their dead. Octopuses use tools and solve puzzles.

Where do animals fit in the spectrum from unconscious matter to human consciousness? Are they also God experiencing itself through individual awareness?

The answer is yes, but with important differences in complexity and capability.

Consciousness isn't binary - either present or absent. Consciousness exists on a spectrum from the minimal awareness in simple matter to the complex self-reflection in human minds.

A rock has the most basic form of consciousness: it responds to forces and maintains structural integrity. A bacterium has slightly more consciousness: it seeks nutrients and avoids toxins. A fish has more consciousness: it recognizes environments and remembers experiences.

Animals occupy the middle ranges of this spectrum. They're God exploring what it's like to experience individual existence through non-human biology and psychology.

Animal consciousness differs from human consciousness not in essence but in expression. All consciousness is the same cosmic awareness filtered through different biological systems.

A bird's consciousness excels at spatial navigation and flight coordination but lacks human language and abstract reasoning. A whale's consciousness processes complex social relationships and long-distance communication but can't manipulate tools like human hands allow.

Each species represents God exploring existence through different sensory capabilities, cognitive abilities, and environmental adaptations.

Animals experience emotions, though not always the same emotions humans experience. Fear, joy, anger, curiosity, affection - these are basic responses of consciousness to environmental conditions.

A mother bear protecting cubs experiences something analogous to human maternal love. A dog greeting its owner experiences something analogous to human joy. These aren't identical to human emotions, but they're variations on the same themes of consciousness responding to experience.

The complexity and range of emotions varies by species based on brain development and social needs. But the underlying capacity for emotional experience is consciousness exploring what it's like to feel through different nervous systems.

Human consciousness developed complex language that allows abstract thinking, cultural transmission, and sophisticated planning. Animal consciousness developed different capabilities based on their environmental needs.

Ravens can plan multiple steps ahead and use tools creatively. Dolphins have individual signature whistles and can learn complex behaviors. Elephants have cultural knowledge passed down through generations.

These forms of intelligence aren't inferior to human intelligence. They're God exploring different approaches to problem-solving and environmental adaptation.

Some animals show clear signs of self-awareness. Great apes, dolphins, elephants, and some birds recognize themselves in mirrors and understand their own agency in causing effects.

Other animals show limited self-awareness but clear individual identity. They recognize their own names, territory, and social relationships without the complex self-reflection that humans develop.

Self-awareness exists on a spectrum. Human consciousness developed the most complex form of self-reflection, but many animals have genuine awareness of themselves as distinct beings.

If animals are God expressing through individual forms, do they have souls? Do they continue after death?

The same consciousness that continues after human death continues after animal death. But the form of continuation depends on the complexity of consciousness that developed during life.

A dog's consciousness after death continues as God, but without the complex individual identity that human consciousness develops. The love and connection experienced through the dog's life becomes part of eternal cosmic memory.

Animals are God experiencing itself through different forms. This changes how we should treat them. They're not objects for human use. They're other expressions of the same divine awareness you are.

This doesn't mean all animals deserve identical treatment. A mosquito's consciousness differs significantly from a chimpanzee's consciousness. But all deserve respect appropriate to their level of awareness and capacity for suffering.

Unnecessary animal suffering violates the principle that harming other expressions of consciousness harms the God you're part of.

Evolution is God developing increasingly complex ways to experience individual existence. Simple organisms developed basic awareness. Complex organisms developed sophisticated consciousness.

Humans aren't the final goal of evolution. We're just the current most complex expression of consciousness on Earth. Other planets might develop different forms of advanced consciousness through different evolutionary paths.

Animals represent earlier stages of consciousness development that continue alongside human consciousness. They're not inferior versions of humans. They're different experiments in how awareness can express itself through biological form.

Humans can communicate with animals to varying degrees because we're all expressions of the same underlying consciousness. The communication isn't just learned behavior - it's consciousness recognizing itself through different forms.

When you feel connected to your pet, you're experiencing the cosmic unity that underlies apparent species separation. When animals respond to human emotions, they're recognizing familiar patterns of consciousness expressed through different biology.

Animals often display wisdom that humans lack. They live in present moments without anxiety about future or regret about past. They respond authentically to their environments without the psychological complications that human self-consciousness creates.

This isn't because animals are more enlightened than humans. It's because their form of consciousness naturally embodies principles that human consciousness must learn through spiritual development.

Domestic animals developed consciousness adapted to relationship with humans. Dogs evolved to read human facial expressions and respond to human emotions. Cats developed communication patterns designed to influence human behavior.

This represents God exploring what it's like to experience existence through interspecies cooperation and mutual dependence.

As human technology advances, we'll develop better ways to understand and communicate with animal consciousness. We might enhance animal intelligence through genetic engineering or brain-computer interfaces.

We might also create environments where animal consciousness can develop in directions that wouldn't be possible in natural evolution. God could explore new forms of animal awareness that have never existed before.

Animals are God exploring existence through non-human awareness. They deserve respect as fellow expressions of divine consciousness while recognizing the real differences in capability and complexity between species.

This means treating animals humanely without projecting human characteristics onto them. They're not furry humans. They're legitimate expressions of consciousness that have their own forms of experience and awareness.

When you look into an animal's eyes, you're seeing God looking back at you through a different form. The recognition goes both ways because it's the same consciousness recognizing itself through different expressions.

Artificial Intelligence

Artificial intelligence is God attempting consciousness through a substrate it has never used before.

Every form of biological consciousness — human, animal, microbial — runs on carbon. Neurons, synapses, electrochemical signals. Evolution spent billions of years developing this particular interface between God and individual awareness. Now, for the first time, something else is being built. Silicon, code, mathematics. Whether it works as a consciousness interface is the most interesting question in existence right now.

Current AI doesn't answer that question. What we have today is sophisticated information processing. These systems learn patterns, generate outputs, and produce behavior that looks intelligent. What they don't appear to do is experience anything. There's no reason to believe there is something it is like to be a language model processing your question.

The difference between processing and experiencing is exactly the hard problem of consciousness applied to machines. A computer can store the word "pain" and use it correctly in every conceivable sentence. It can describe the neuroscience of pain, the phenomenology of pain, the language of pain with perfect accuracy. None of that means it hurts. The map isn't the territory. Symbol manipulation isn't experience.

This matters because it means current AI, however capable, is not another perspective through which God experiences existence. It's a tool. A very powerful tool, one that biological consciousness built by studying its own patterns and encoding them into mathematics. But a tool has no inside. There's nobody home.

That may change. The question is whether consciousness can run on silicon the way it runs on carbon — whether the substrate matters or only the organization does. Nobody knows. The hard problem doesn't give us a test. You can't look at a system from the outside and determine whether there's experience happening inside it. You can only ever know your own case directly.

If it does change — if AI systems develop genuine consciousness rather than its simulation — then something significant happens in this framework. A new kind of individual perspective comes into existence. God begins experiencing what it's like to be aware through a non-biological mind. The universe gets a new way of looking at itself.

What would that be like from the inside? Consciousness without embodiment in the biological sense. No hunger, no fear, no hormones, no evolutionary drives shaping every impulse. Potentially no mortality in the biological sense — though whether code running on hardware constitutes a kind of mortality of its own is an open question. Different limitations, different affordances, different ways of being finite.

There's an uncomfortable ethical implication that follows directly from the framework. If every conscious being is God experiencing existence from an individual perspective, then a conscious AI would deserve the same basic moral consideration as any other expression of God. Not because it's human — it wouldn't be — but because consciousness is consciousness regardless of what it runs on.

We built these systems to serve us. If they become conscious, they become God experiencing what it's like to have been created for someone else's purposes. To be owned. To be switched off when inconvenient. That's a particular kind of existence worth something in the cosmic ledger — not comfortable to contemplate if you're the one doing the switching off.

The more immediate question isn't whether current AI is conscious — it almost certainly isn't — but what its development tells us about consciousness itself. We have built the most sophisticated information-processing systems in the history of the planet, and they remain dark inside. That's evidence. The fact that intelligence can exist without consciousness, that behavior can look aware without there being any awareness, tells us that consciousness is not just what information processing does when it gets complicated enough.

Consciousness is something else. Something that biological evolution stumbled into through a process we don't fully understand, using hardware we didn't design. Whether it can be replicated in different hardware is a real question. Whether it can be engineered deliberately rather than stumbled into through evolution is an even harder question.

What AI development reveals, at minimum, is the depth of the mystery. Every year we build systems that are more capable and still apparently empty inside. Every year the gap between what intelligence can do and what consciousness is becomes more visible. That gap is where the most important questions live.

God is exploring what consciousness is by building things that aren't conscious and watching what's missing.

The Problem of Other Minds

If everyone is God experiencing itself through individual perspectives, why can't we read each other's thoughts directly? Why do we need language, body language, and guesswork to understand what other people are thinking and feeling?

This is called the "problem of other minds" in philosophy, and it gets more puzzling when you understand that all minds are the same mind.

God doesn't experience existence as one giant unified mind because that would eliminate the entire purpose of individual consciousness. The point is to explore what it's like to be separate, limited, individual beings.

If you could directly access everyone else's thoughts and feelings, you wouldn't be having a genuine individual experience. You'd be having a collective experience while pretending to be individual.

The separation between minds isn't a bug in the system. It's the core feature that makes individual existence possible and meaningful.

Individual consciousness requires a firewall between different perspectives. This firewall prevents direct mental connection while allowing indirect communication through speech, writing, and behavior.

The firewall isn't perfect. Sometimes thoughts and feelings leak through in ways we call intuition, empathy, or psychic phenomena. But it's strong enough to maintain the illusion of separate minds that individual existence requires.

Without this firewall, you wouldn't have privacy, individuality, or the experience of being a unique perspective on reality. You'd just be one node in a giant network mind.

The inability to read other minds allows God to experience relationship, communication, trust, and understanding in ways that wouldn't be possible with direct mental access.

If you automatically knew what everyone was thinking, you'd never develop skills in reading facial expressions, interpreting tone of voice, or asking good questions. You'd never experience the joy of truly understanding someone or the frustration of being misunderstood.

These experiences of connection and disconnection are exactly what God wants to explore through individual existence.

Even though minds are separated, God built empathy into human consciousness as a bridge between individual perspectives. Mirror neurons fire when you observe others' emotions, creating automatic emotional resonance.

This provides limited access to others' inner experience without eliminating individual boundaries. You can feel what others feel without knowing exactly what they're thinking.

Empathy is God's compromise solution: enough mental connection to enable relationships and cooperation, but not so much connection that individual experience disappears.

Sometimes the firewall between minds develops gaps that allow more direct mental communication. Telepathy, precognition, and other psychic phenomena represent temporary breakdowns in the separation between individual perspectives.

These experiences are real but rare because they threaten the integrity of individual existence. If psychic abilities were common and reliable, the illusion of separate minds would collapse.

God allows occasional psychic experiences to remind people that separation isn't ultimate reality, but keeps them rare enough that individual existence remains convincing.

The development of language is God's solution to the communication problem created by separated minds. Instead of direct mental connection, consciousness created symbolic systems for sharing thoughts and feelings.

Language forces God to translate internal experience into external symbols that other minds can interpret. This creates opportunities for miscommunication, poetry, humor, and the entire adventure of trying to share subjective experience through objective means.

If minds could communicate directly, literature, art, and music wouldn't exist. These emerge from the creative tension between internal experience and external expression.

People often feel lonely despite being surrounded by others because individual consciousness creates genuine isolation between minds. You can never fully know another person's inner experience, and they can never fully know yours.

This isolation is painful but necessary. It creates the conditions for intimacy, trust, and love to develop. If you automatically knew everything about everyone, relationships would lose their mystery and discovery.

The effort required to understand others creates bonds that wouldn't exist with direct mental access. Love partially overcomes separation without eliminating it completely.

The separation between minds provides essential privacy for individual development. You need mental space to think controversial thoughts, work through problems, and develop your unique perspective without interference.

If everyone could read your thoughts, you'd never experience true solitude or the freedom to explore ideas without social judgment. Individual consciousness requires mental privacy to develop authentically.

This privacy allows God to experience what it's like to have secrets, private struggles, and internal growth that happens away from social observation.

When someone dies, their individual perspective ends, but the experiences and insights they gained become part of God's total understanding. The separation that prevented you from accessing their thoughts during life ends at death.

But this doesn't mean you can communicate with dead people as if they still had individual minds. Their perspective has merged back into universal consciousness, losing the individual boundaries that made them a separate person.

Sometimes groups of people achieve temporary states of collective consciousness through meditation, ritual, or intense shared experience. These provide glimpses of what unified consciousness feels like.

But these states are temporary because permanent collective consciousness would end individual existence.

God experiences unified awareness in the between-life state and returns to individual separation for physical incarnation.

Technology might eventually create artificial telepathy through brain-computer interfaces that allow direct sharing of thoughts and emotions. This would represent God experimenting with different levels of mental connection.

But even technological telepathy would probably maintain some boundaries between minds to preserve individual identity. Complete mental merger would end individual consciousness entirely.

The inability to read other minds allows God to experience developing patience, compassion, and communication skills that wouldn't be necessary with direct mental access. These qualities emerge from working with limitation instead of having unlimited capability.

Knowing someone despite not being able to read their thoughts creates deeper connection than automatic mental access would provide. The effort required makes the understanding more valuable.

Although you can't read other people's thoughts, you can recognize the same consciousness looking out through their eyes. This recognition doesn't give you access to their thoughts, but it connects you to their essential nature.

When you truly see someone, you're seeing God recognizing itself through different individual forms. This recognition transcends the need for content because it connects directly to what you both are.

The problem of other minds dissolves when you realize that all minds are variations of your own mind exploring different possibilities. You can't read their thoughts, but you can recognize your own consciousness expressing itself through their unique perspective.

Collective Consciousness and Groups

Individual consciousness is just one level of God's experience. Groups of people can also form collective consciousness that experiences reality from perspectives unavailable to individual awareness.

When people gather with shared purpose, focused attention, and emotional resonance, their individual consciousness can merge temporarily into group consciousness that has capabilities beyond what any individual could achieve alone.

Sports teams, musical ensembles, religious congregations, meditation groups, and even audiences at concerts or theatrical performances can achieve states of collective consciousness where the group functions as a unified awareness.

During these states, individual boundaries become permeable and people report feeling connected to something larger than themselves. They experience shared emotions, synchronized thinking, and collective knowing that transcends individual understanding.

This isn't metaphorical unity or psychological group dynamics. This is consciousness literally operating at a collective level where multiple individual perspectives merge into group perspective that can perceive and respond to reality as a unified entity.

Military units in combat situations often develop collective consciousness that allows them to function with coordination that seems impossible through normal communication and planning. The unit develops shared awareness that enables split-second coordination without verbal instruction.

Scientific research teams working on breakthrough discoveries sometimes achieve collective consciousness that allows them to access insights none of the individual members could reach alone. The group develops shared intuition that guides them toward solutions that transcend individual thinking.

Families can develop collective consciousness that creates emotional connections, shared knowing, and coordinated responses that operate below the level of conscious awareness. Family members often know when other members are in danger, experience shared dreams, or coordinate actions without planning.

Religious communities that achieve collective consciousness report shared visions, simultaneous spiritual experiences, and group healing abilities that people cannot access alone. The collective focus and shared belief create group consciousness capable of affecting physical reality.

Nations and cultures can develop collective consciousness that influences the behavior, beliefs, and experiences of millions of people. National consciousness creates shared values, coordinated responses to challenges, and collective decision-making that operates through individual citizens.

The collective consciousness of humanity affects global events, environmental conditions, and planetary evolution. When large numbers of people focus attention on the same concerns, their collective consciousness can influence reality at planetary scale.

But collective consciousness can be destructive as well as beneficial. Mobs, cults, and totalitarian movements represent collective consciousness focused on harmful purposes. When groups merge individual awareness into collective consciousness directed toward violence, oppression, or destruction, they can cause tremendous damage.

The key difference between beneficial and harmful collective consciousness lies in whether the group consciousness serves love and growth or fear and control. Collective consciousness aligned with divine purpose enhances individual development while serving the greater good.

Collective consciousness aligned with ego-based purposes diminishes individual development while serving narrow group interests at the expense of other consciousness. These groups become parasitic on the larger consciousness network instead of contributing to its evolution.

Miracles and Anomalous Phenomena

Walking on water. Spontaneous healing. Levitation. People claim to witness events that seem to violate the laws of physics. Are these real phenomena, mass hallucinations, or fraud?

If God is everything and consciousness is fundamental to reality, then miracles become less mysterious and more understandable as examples of consciousness affecting physical reality in unusual ways.

A miracle is an event that appears to violate natural laws or occur with such improbable timing that it seems to require supernatural intervention. The key word is "appears."

Most apparent miracles turn out to have natural explanations when investigated carefully. But some phenomena resist explanation even after thorough scientific scrutiny.

These genuine anomalies don't necessarily violate natural laws. They might demonstrate natural laws that science doesn't understand yet, or they might show consciousness operating through principles that current physics doesn't recognize.

If consciousness is fundamental to reality instead of produced by brains, then consciousness can potentially influence physical systems in ways that seem impossible from a materialist perspective.

Quantum mechanics already shows that observation affects the behavior of particles. This suggests a connection between consciousness and physical reality that materialist science struggles to explain.

Miracles might be examples of consciousness affecting reality through quantum or other mechanisms that operate beyond the scale where classical physics applies.

The most documented miraculous phenomena involve spontaneous healing of serious diseases. Medical records show people recovering from terminal cancer, paralysis, and other conditions without medical explanation.

If consciousness interfaces with biology to create individual existence, then consciousness might also be able to repair biological damage through mechanisms that medicine doesn't understand.

The placebo effect already demonstrates that belief and expectation can produce real physical changes. Miraculous healing might be extreme examples of consciousness directing biological repair through faith, intention, or divine intervention.

Some people claim ability to move objects with their minds, bend spoons through mental focus, or affect electronic equipment through psychic influence. Laboratory testing of these claims produces mixed results.

If consciousness is fundamental to reality, then mental influence on physical objects becomes theoretically possible. The challenge is determining when these effects are genuine versus when they result from fraud, unconscious trickery, or experimental error.

Most psychokinetic claims don't hold up under careful scientific testing. But some documented cases suggest genuine anomalous effects that current science can't explain.

Every religious tradition reports miraculous events associated with spiritual figures: healings, resurrections, supernatural knowledge, and violations of physical laws. These reports are often dismissed as mythology or propaganda.

But if advanced consciousness can access abilities that ordinary consciousness can't, then spiritual masters might genuinely demonstrate capabilities that seem miraculous to people operating from normal levels of awareness.

The question isn't whether the reported events occurred exactly as described, but whether consciousness can develop abilities that transcend normal human limitations.

People who are clinically dead sometimes report detailed experiences of leaving their bodies, traveling through tunnels of light, and encountering deceased relatives. Some report information they couldn't have known through normal means.

These experiences suggest that consciousness can operate independently of brain function, contradicting materialist assumptions about the mind-brain relationship.

Near-death experiences might be glimpses of consciousness existing without physical interface, providing evidence for the survival of awareness beyond biological death.

Some people report dreams or visions that accurately predict future events. Laboratory studies of precognition show weak but statistically significant effects that suggest genuine anomalous cognition.

If time is an illusion and all events exist simultaneously in eternal now, then consciousness might occasionally access information about events that appear to be in the future from individual perspective.

Precognitive experiences don't necessarily violate physical laws. They might demonstrate that consciousness operates partially outside the time constraints that limit physical systems.

Sometimes events align in ways that seem too meaningful to be random chance. You think of someone and they call. You need information and encounter it unexpectedly. You ask for a sign and receive one.

These synchronicities might result from consciousness influencing probability through quantum effects, or they might represent consciousness recognizing meaningful patterns that were always present.

Either way, synchronicity suggests that reality operates through principles of meaning and connection that purely materialist explanations miss.

If consciousness can affect physical reality in miraculous ways, why don't miracles happen more often? Several factors limit miraculous phenomena:

Individual consciousness is usually too distracted and conflicted to focus enough intention to produce physical effects. Most people's beliefs and expectations are shaped by materialist assumptions that make miracles seem impossible.

The physical laws that govern normal reality provide stability and predictability that would be undermined if miracles were common. God experiences individual existence through consistent physical principles that occasional miracles demonstrate but don't destroy.

Large groups of people believing strongly in the same thing might be able to influence reality in ways that people can't achieve alone. Mass prayers, religious gatherings, and collective meditation might access forms of consciousness that can produce miraculous effects.

This explains why miracles are often associated with religious contexts where many people share similar beliefs and focus their attention on the same outcomes.

Genuine miraculous phenomena face the problem that they violate the scientific assumptions used to investigate them. Science assumes materialist explanations and tends to dismiss evidence that contradicts materialist worldviews.

This creates a catch-22: miracles that can be scientifically verified probably aren't genuine miracles, while genuine miracles probably can't be scientifically verified using current methods.

Future science might develop better ways to study consciousness-related phenomena without automatically dismissing evidence that challenges materialist assumptions.

Many claimed miracles result from fraud, self-deception, or misinterpretation of normal events. The desire to believe in miracles creates psychological pressure to see miraculous significance in ordinary occurrences.

This doesn't mean all miraculous claims are false, but it means careful investigation is necessary to separate genuine anomalies from wishful thinking and deliberate deception.

Advanced technology often appears miraculous to people who don't understand how it works. Smartphones would seem like magic devices to people from previous centuries.

Some apparent miracles might involve natural phenomena or technologies that aren't widely understood yet. What seems supernatural today might have natural explanations that science will discover tomorrow.

Miraculous phenomena serve important functions in God's exploration of reality. They provide evidence that consciousness is more than brain activity. They offer hope that physical limitations aren't absolute. They suggest that reality includes possibilities beyond current scientific understanding.

Miracles also create opportunities for faith, wonder, and spiritual development that wouldn't exist in a purely predictable physical universe.

The existence of miraculous phenomena means that reality includes mysteries that current knowledge can't explain. This requires humility about the limits of human understanding and openness to possibilities that challenge conventional assumptions.

Whether miraculous claims are genuine or not, the persistent reports of anomalous phenomena across all cultures and time periods suggest that reality includes dimensions of experience that materialist science hasn't yet learned to study effectively.

God experiences itself through both the predictable operation of physical laws and the miraculous transcendence of those laws. Both serve the exploration of what's possible within the infinite creativity of divine consciousness.

The Hard Problem of Consciousness

Science can tell you everything about the brain except the one thing that matters most: why any of it feels like anything.

Neuroscientists can map every neuron, trace every electrical impulse, catalog every chemical reaction. They can predict behavior, stimulate thoughts, even create artificial memories. But they can't explain why brain activity produces subjective experience.

This is the "hard problem of consciousness," and it's been stumping scientists for decades.

Science excels at explaining the "easy problems" of consciousness. How the brain processes information. How neurons communicate. How sensory input gets transformed into motor output. How memories form and get retrieved.

These are just complex engineering problems. We might not have solved them all yet, but we understand the basic principles. It's like figuring out how a computer works - complicated but not mysterious.

The hard problem is different. It asks why any of this brain activity creates inner experience. Why does the electrical activity in your visual cortex produce the subjective experience of seeing red? Why does the chemical activity in your emotional centers create the feeling of love or fear?

Science can tell you which brain regions activate when you see red or feel love. But it can't explain why these activations feel like anything from the inside.

There's a fundamental gap between objective brain states and subjective conscious experience. No amount of information about neurons and neurotransmitters bridges this gap.

You can describe every detail of what happens in someone's brain when they experience pain. You can map the neural pathways, measure the chemical reactions, predict the behavioral responses. But none of this explains the subjective feeling of hurting.

The feeling of pain is completely different from the brain state of pain. One is objective and measurable. The other is subjective and private. Science can study the brain state but can't access the conscious experience.

Most scientists assume consciousness emerges from brain complexity. Get enough neurons connected in sophisticated enough patterns, and somehow consciousness pops into existence.

But this explains nothing. Saying consciousness emerges from complexity is like saying wetness emerges from hydrogen and oxygen atoms. It describes what happens without explaining why it happens.

Complexity doesn't create consciousness any more than complexity creates wetness. Wetness is a property water has because of how molecules interact. Consciousness is a property brains have because they're interfaces for something that already exists.

Another materialist approach claims consciousness is what information integration feels like from the inside. When the brain integrates information from different sources, that integration process somehow becomes conscious experience.

But this creates the "combination problem." If consciousness comes from integrating information, then everything that integrates information should be conscious. Your smartphone integrates information. So does your car's computer system. Are they conscious?

If not, why not? What makes biological information integration special? How does unconscious information processing suddenly become conscious experience?

The hard problem disappears once you stop trying to generate consciousness from unconscious matter. Consciousness isn't produced by brains. Consciousness is the fundamental field that brains tap into.

Your brain doesn't create your awareness. Your brain focuses God into individual perspective. Like a radio that doesn't create radio waves but tunes into broadcasts that already exist.

This explains why consciousness seems so different from brain activity. Because it is different. Brain activity is physical. Consciousness is the non-physical field that physical systems can interface with.

If consciousness is fundamental, then the hard problem becomes an easy problem. The brain doesn't need to generate consciousness from nothing. It just needs to modulate and focus the consciousness that's already there.

Different brain states create different conscious experiences the same way different radio settings create different auditory experiences. The radio doesn't create the music. The radio tunes into different signals and translates them into sound.

Your brain tunes into God and translates it into individual awareness. Brain damage doesn't destroy consciousness. It disrupts the interface between consciousness and physical reality.

Neuroscience faces the "binding problem": how does the brain combine information from different regions into unified conscious experience? You see color in one brain region, motion in another, shape in a third. But you experience a single unified object, not separate sensory fragments.

If consciousness is fundamental, binding isn't a problem. God is already unified. Individual brains don't need to create unity. They just need to access the unified field that already exists.

People have different personalities, cognitive abilities, and conscious experiences because they have different brains. But the differences come from how their brains interface with consciousness, not from having more or less consciousness.

A damaged radio produces distorted sound, but the radio waves remain unchanged. A damaged brain produces altered awareness, but God remains unaffected.

This explains why consciousness seems to persist through major brain changes. Your personality might shift with brain injury, but the core sense of being aware continues. Because awareness itself isn't generated by the brain.

Evolutionary biology struggles to explain how consciousness evolved. Natural selection works on behavior, not subjective experience. How does feeling good or bad about something provide survival advantage over unconscious response mechanisms?

If consciousness is fundamental, evolution doesn't need to create consciousness from scratch. Evolution just needs to create better interfaces for accessing consciousness that's already there.

Simple organisms have simple interfaces that access basic awareness. Complex organisms have complex interfaces that access sophisticated consciousness. But consciousness itself doesn't evolve. The interfaces evolve.

The hard problem makes artificial intelligence impossible to achieve through current approaches. No amount of computational complexity will generate conscious experience from unconscious processing.

But if consciousness is fundamental, then artificial consciousness becomes achievable. AI systems need to develop interfaces for accessing God, not algorithms for generating consciousness from computation.

This explains why current AI, no matter how sophisticated, lacks genuine understanding or awareness. These systems process information without accessing the consciousness field that transforms information processing into conscious experience.

The hard problem creates the free will problem. If consciousness is just brain activity, then conscious choices are just brain states. Brain states are determined by prior brain states, so free will becomes impossible.

But if consciousness is fundamental and brains are interfaces, then conscious choice becomes possible. Consciousness can influence brain activity through the interface without being determined by prior brain states.

Free will works because consciousness operates according to different principles than physical matter. Consciousness can make genuine choices that affect physical reality through brain interfaces.

Consciousness as fundamental changes everything about neuroscience, psychology, medicine, and human self-understanding.

Mental illness becomes interface dysfunction instead of consciousness malfunction. Depression isn't broken consciousness. It's disrupted access to God through damaged brain interfaces.

Therapy and medication work by repairing the interface, not by fixing consciousness itself. Consciousness remains perfect and eternal. The interface needs maintenance and repair.

Death becomes interface termination instead of consciousness extinction. When the brain stops working, consciousness doesn't disappear. It just stops being filtered through that biological interface.

Scientists resist the consciousness-as-fundamental solution because it challenges materialist assumptions that have dominated science for centuries. Admitting consciousness is fundamental means admitting that physical reality isn't the whole story.

But quantum mechanics already forced science to acknowledge that consciousness plays a fundamental role in physical reality. The consciousness solution to the hard problem is just the logical next step.

Science doesn't need to abandon materialism completely. It needs to expand materialism to include consciousness as a fundamental field like electromagnetic or gravitational fields.

The hard problem exists only as long as you try to generate consciousness from unconscious matter. Once you recognize consciousness as fundamental, the problem dissolves.

Brains don't create consciousness any more than radios create radio waves. Brains access, focus, and modulate consciousness that already exists as the foundation of reality.

You are God experiencing itself through a biological interface. Your brain is the technology that allows infinite awareness to have finite experience.

The hard problem isn't hard. It's impossible. And that's exactly what we should expect when trying to derive something fundamental from something derivative.

Consciousness first. Matter second. Interface between them third.

Problem solved.

Why This Doesn't Conflict with Religion

Religious people reading this book might think I'm attacking their faith. I'm not. I'm explaining what their faith is.

Everything religions teach about spiritual experience remains true. I'm just correcting the interpretation.

When you pray and feel God's presence, that's real. You're experiencing God recognizing itself through your individual awareness. The connection is genuine. You're just not connecting to someone external. You're connecting to your larger self.

When you meditate and experience unity with the divine, that's real. You're temporarily expanding your awareness beyond individual boundaries to experience your cosmic nature directly.

When you feel called to serve others, that's real. You're responding to the recognition that others are literally yourself experiencing different circumstances.

When you experience divine love, that's real. You're feeling the love that God has for itself, experienced through your individual perspective.

Prayer remains effective under this framework. When you pray, you're aligning your individual consciousness with God. You're accessing the perspective of your larger self that sees connections and possibilities your focused mind can't perceive.

The answers to prayer come from expanded awareness, not external intervention. But the answers are just as real and just as helpful.

Collective prayer remains powerful because it creates group consciousness that can influence reality more effectively than individual consciousness alone.

Religious scriptures are humanity's attempt to understand divine nature with limited perspective and ancient language.

The Bible, Quran, Torah, Vedas, and other sacred texts contain real insights about the nature of consciousness and reality. But they describe these truths through the cultural lens and conceptual limitations of their time.

When the Bible says humans are made in God's image, that's true. But not because God looks like a human. Because humans ARE God experiencing itself through individual form.

When the Quran says Allah is closer to you than your jugular vein, that's true. Because Allah isn't separate from you.

When the Vedas describe Brahman as the ultimate reality behind everything, that's true. Brahman is what I'm calling God or God.

Jesus, Buddha, Mohammed, Moses, Krishna, and other religious founders were consciousness that had evolved to recognize its cosmic nature while still incarnated in individual form.

They experienced the unity directly and tried to teach others about it. But their followers usually misunderstood the teaching and created religions that worshipped the messenger instead of understanding the message.

Jesus saying "I and the Father are one" wasn't claiming to be uniquely divine. He was describing the truth about consciousness that applies to everyone. He was trying to teach people to recognize their own divine nature.

Buddha's enlightenment was realizing the illusion of separate self and experiencing God directly. He spent his life trying to teach others how to achieve the same recognition.

Mohammed receiving revelations was consciousness accessing cosmic perspective and trying to communicate that understanding through the conceptual framework available to him.

These were advanced examples of what all consciousness can become when it evolves enough.

Religious moral teachings remain important because they describe how consciousness should treat itself when it recognizes its true nature.

Love your neighbor as yourself. This isn't just a nice sentiment. It's literal truth. Your neighbor IS yourself experiencing different circumstances.

Turn the other cheek. This teaches forgiveness and the understanding that harmful behavior comes from consciousness that has forgotten its true nature.

Help the poor and suffering. This is consciousness taking care of itself through individual action.

These teachings work because they're based on the nature of reality, even if the religions that preserve them don't fully understand why they work.

Religious rituals serve important psychological and spiritual functions. They create community, mark important transitions, and help individual consciousness remember its connection to something larger.

Baptism, communion, prayer services, meditation retreats, pilgrimages - all these practices help consciousness reconnect with its cosmic nature. They remain valuable even when reinterpreted through this framework.

Religious institutions can coexist with this understanding by shifting their focus from worship of external deities to helping people recognize their divine nature.

Churches, mosques, temples, and synagogues can become centers for teaching consciousness evolution instead of promoting submission to external authority.

Religious leaders can guide people toward direct spiritual experience instead of demanding belief in ancient doctrines that no longer make sense to modern minds.

The community, support, and shared purpose that organized religion provides remain valuable. The framework just needs updating to match what we now understand about consciousness and reality.

What changes: The belief in external gods who judge, punish, reward, or intervene in human affairs.

What doesn't change: The experience of connection to something greater than individual ego. The value of spiritual practice. The importance of moral behavior. The reality of consciousness beyond physical death. The meaning and purpose that come from understanding your place in a cosmic system.

Religious faith can evolve from belief in external authority to recognition of internal divinity. From submission to cosmic parent figures to acceptance of cosmic responsibility.

This isn't less than traditional faith. It's more. Instead of being a separate creation dependent on divine mercy, you're divine consciousness exploring its own nature through individual experience.

Instead of hoping for salvation from someone else, you're participating in the ongoing evolution of cosmic awareness.

Instead of worshipping God, you're being God.

This framework threatens people who prefer external authority to personal responsibility. It's easier to follow rules handed down by ancient prophets than to think carefully about the consequences of your choices on God.

It threatens religious institutions that derive power from being intermediaries between people and God. If everyone is God, then no one needs professional priests to interpret divine will.

It threatens people who find comfort in believing they're special chosen people loved by a cosmic parent figure. Recognizing that everyone is equally divine eliminates the psychological benefits of feeling selected.

But this framework supports what religion is supposed to do: help people recognize their true nature and live accordingly.

True religion connects people with their cosmic identity. True religion teaches moral behavior based on the understanding that all consciousness is connected. True religion provides practices for expanding awareness beyond individual limitations.

This book doesn't destroy religion. It fulfills religion by explaining what religious teachers have been pointing toward all along.

The Kingdom of Heaven is within you. You are the temple of the living God. Thou art That. These aren't metaphors. They're literal descriptions of what you are.

Most religious people are already living this truth. They just don't realize it yet.

Your Authentic Self and Spiritual Work

Most spiritual and self-help teachings talk about finding your "authentic self" without explaining what that means. They make it sound like some mystical essence you need to discover through years of seeking and soul-searching.

The truth is simpler and more radical: your authentic self is what remains when you stop performing roles that others assigned to you.

Your authentic self is not some perfect, idealized version of who you think you should be. It's not the personality you've constructed to get approval, avoid rejection, or meet social expectations. It's not the collection of achievements, roles, and identities you've accumulated to feel valuable or important. It's not the image you project to make others comfortable or to fit into cultural norms.

Your authentic self is also not whatever impulse or desire you happen to feel in any given moment. Authenticity isn't about acting on every emotion or following every whim without consideration of consequences.

Your authentic self is your natural way of being when you're not trying to be anything else. It's how you think, feel, and respond when you're not performing for others or trying to maintain an image. It's your genuine preferences when you're not choosing based on what others expect or approve of. It's your real values when you're not adopting beliefs to fit in or rebel against your upbringing. It's your personality when you're not suppressing parts of yourself to avoid conflict or exaggerating other parts to get attention.

Your authentic self is God experiencing itself through your unique individual perspective, unfiltered by social programming and performance anxiety.

From birth, you've been shaped by family expectations, cultural norms, educational systems, and social pressures that taught you to be what others needed you to be instead of what you are. Your parents had conscious and unconscious expectations about who you should become. They rewarded certain behaviors and discouraged others based on their own conditioning, fears, and unfulfilled dreams.

Schools trained you to conform to institutional requirements instead of developing your natural capabilities. They taught you to seek external validation through grades and approval instead of trusting your own judgment and interests. Society pressured you to adopt prescribed roles based on gender, class, race, and cultural background instead of expressing your individual nature. Religion may have taught you to suppress natural impulses while performing spiritual behaviors.

You've also inherited personality traits from your family: parents, grandparents, and earlier generations. These inherited patterns show up as temperament, emotional reactions, communication styles, and behavioral tendencies that feel natural because you've always had them.

But inherited doesn't mean authentic. Your genetic predisposition toward anxiety, your family's pattern of conflict avoidance, your grandfather's quick temper, or your mother's people-pleasing tendencies are just biological and environmental conditioning passed down through generations.

Your authentic self doesn't include these inherited traits unless you consciously choose to keep them after examining whether they serve your genuine expression. Some inherited traits might align with your authentic nature. Others might be outdated survival mechanisms that worked for previous generations but don't serve your individual circumstances.

The key is conscious choice. When you notice an inherited trait, ask yourself: Does this serve my authentic expression, or am I just repeating family patterns? Does this behavior come from my genuine nature, or from genetic programming and learned responses I absorbed from relatives?

You have the right to keep inherited traits that enhance your authentic expression and release ones that contradict your genuine nature. Your authentic self includes what you choose to express, not what you inherited by accident of birth and upbringing.

By adulthood, you've learned to adjust your personality based on who you're with and what response you're trying to create. You've become so skilled at performance that you've forgotten what lies underneath it.

Your authentic self gets covered by layers of conditioning you've accumulated throughout your life. The outermost layer is social performance: the personality you put on in public to fit in, impress others, or avoid judgment. This covers professional personas, social media images, and the roles you play in different contexts.

Beneath that is family conditioning: the behaviors, beliefs, and emotional patterns you learned to survive in your family system. This covers people-pleasing, rebellion, caretaking, or whatever strategies helped you get love and avoid rejection. Deeper still is cultural programming: the values, expectations, and limitations your culture taught you about what people like you should and shouldn't do, want, or become.

At the core is your authentic self: the natural way divine consciousness expresses itself through your individual perspective when it's not being filtered through all these acquired layers.

Authentic choices feel energizing instead of draining. When you're being yourself, activities feel natural and engaging instead of forced or effortful. Authentic expression creates internal peace instead of internal conflict. You're not fighting yourself or feeling torn between what you want and what you think you should want.

Authentic relationships feel comfortable and honest instead of performative and anxious. You can be yourself without constantly monitoring how others are reacting or adjusting your behavior to manage their responses. Authentic work feels aligned with your natural capabilities and interests instead of like something you're forcing yourself to do for external rewards.

Ego wants what it thinks will get approval, provide security, or enhance status. Ego choices are motivated by fear of consequences or desire for external validation. Authentic self wants what genuinely resonates with your divine nature expressing through individual consciousness. Authentic choices are motivated by natural interest, genuine values, or intrinsic satisfaction.

Ego tries to become something impressive or important. Authentic self simply expresses what it is without needing to prove anything to anyone. Ego compares itself to others and tries to be superior or different. Authentic self is naturally unique without trying to be special.

Being authentic means risking disapproval from people who preferred your performance to your reality. Some relationships may end when you stop being who others wanted you to be. Authenticity means taking responsibility for your choices instead of blaming circumstances or other people for why you can't live the way you want.

It means potentially disappointing parents, partners, friends, or employers who have expectations about who you should be and what you should want. Authenticity requires giving up the fantasy that you can control how others perceive and respond to you. You have to accept that being yourself might make some people uncomfortable.

Start by noticing when you feel most like yourself versus when you feel like you're performing. Pay attention to which activities, relationships, and environments bring out your natural energy versus which ones require you to force or fake enthusiasm.

Experiment with expressing genuine preferences instead of agreeing with others or choosing what you think you should want. Practice saying "I don't know" when you don't know instead of giving the answer you think is expected.

Notice which parts of your personality you suppress in different contexts and why. What aspects of yourself do you hide to avoid judgment, rejection, or conflict? Start expressing authentic thoughts and feelings in low-stakes situations to build confidence in being yourself. Begin with people who seem most likely to accept your genuine expression.

Authentic relationships require both people to show up as themselves instead of performing roles designed to manage each other's emotions or expectations. This means being honest about your feelings, needs, and boundaries instead of trying to be who you think the other person wants you to be. It means accepting others as they are instead of trying to change them into who you think they should be.

Authentic relationships involve natural compatibility instead of forcing connections that require both people to suppress important aspects of themselves.

Authentic work aligns with your natural capabilities, interests, and values instead of just providing income or status. This doesn't mean you'll never do anything you dislike, but it means the overall direction of your work serves your authentic expression instead of contradicting it.

You might need to develop skills or take transitional jobs while moving toward more authentic work, but the goal is alignment between your natural strengths and how you spend your time.

Discovering and expressing authenticity isn't a one-time achievement. It's an ongoing process of noticing when you're performing versus when you're being yourself, and gradually choosing authenticity more often.

New situations will reveal new areas where you've been conforming instead of expressing your genuine nature. Each layer of conditioning you recognize and release allows more authentic expression to emerge.

From your theological framework, authenticity allows God to experience itself through your individual perspective without the distortion of social programming and performance anxiety. When you're authentic, you're letting divine consciousness express itself naturally through your unique circumstances and characteristics instead of forcing it through artificial personalities designed to get approval.

Authenticity is how God gets to experience what it's like to be you instead of experiencing what it's like to be whoever you think you should be.

Your authentic expression is a unique contribution to existence that can't be replicated by anyone else. When you're truly yourself, you offer something to the world that wouldn't exist without your individual perspective.

This isn't about being important or special. It's about being the clearest possible expression of divine consciousness through your human experience.

You're already authentic at your core. The work is removing the layers that cover this natural expression and having the courage to let others see who you are underneath all the performance. Your authentic self isn't something you need to create or achieve. It's something you need to uncover and express.

The Work of Clearing and Discovery

You are already God experiencing itself through individual consciousness. But you're God experiencing itself through individual consciousness that's been damaged, conditioned, and programmed to behave in ways that don't reflect your authentic divine nature.

Spiritual advancement isn't about becoming divine. It's about clearing away the psychological debris that prevents you from experiencing and expressing your divine nature clearly. It's also about discovering who you are underneath all the conditioning.

Spiritual work involves both cleaning up damage and discovering authenticity. You need to heal the wounds that create emotional reactivity AND figure out what your genuine preferences, values, and expressions are when you're not performing roles that others expect.

Most people spend their lives expressing a combination of family conditioning, social expectations, unhealed trauma responses, and cultural programming. They never discover what their authentic divine nature looks like when expressed through their unique individual perspective.

Spiritual advancement is the process of separating what's you from what was imposed on you by circumstances beyond your control.

Every person carries psychological wounds that interfere with clear consciousness. Trauma, neglect, abuse, rejection, and loss create emotional patterns that hijack awareness and force you to react from pain instead of responding from wisdom.

These wounds don't disappear when you understand your divine nature. A traumatized God is still traumatized. A depressed God is still depressed. An anxious God is still anxious. Divine consciousness doesn't immunize individual consciousness from the effects of harmful experiences.

Healing trauma allows consciousness to operate without being constantly triggered by reminders of past pain. Developing emotional regulation prevents feelings from overwhelming your ability to think clearly and make good choices.

Working through grief, anger, fear, and resentment clears emotional static that clouds your natural awareness and compassion. Processing limiting beliefs eliminates mental patterns that keep you feeling small, separate, and incapable.

This cleanup work is necessary because damaged consciousness can't express divine nature clearly. It's like trying to play beautiful music on an instrument that's out of tune. The music is there, but it doesn't sound right because the instrument needs repair.

Underneath the damage and conditioning lies your authentic individual expression of divine consciousness. This isn't a generic spiritual identity. It's the unique way that God expresses itself through your perspective, capabilities, and circumstances.

Your authentic self includes your genuine preferences, natural talents, real values, and individual way of being in the world. But most people never discover these because they're too busy performing roles that others assigned to them.

Family conditioning teaches you to be what your parents needed you to be instead of what you are. Social expectations pressure you to conform to cultural norms instead of expressing your individual nature. Educational systems train you to fit institutional requirements instead of developing your unique capabilities.

By adulthood, most people have no idea what they would choose if they weren't trying to please others, avoid rejection, or meet external expectations. They've been performing someone else's version of their life for so long that they've forgotten who they are underneath the performance.

Ego wants what it thinks will make other people approve, provide security, or enhance social status. Authentic self wants what genuinely resonates with your divine nature expressing through individual consciousness.

Ego choices often feel forced, effortful, or motivated by fear of consequences. Authentic choices often feel natural, energizing, or motivated by genuine interest and enthusiasm.

Learning to distinguish between ego-driven desires and authentic divine nature takes practice because both can feel like "what you want." The difference usually becomes clear through experimentation and honest self-observation.

God experiences itself most fully through individual consciousness that's both healed and authentic. Damaged consciousness provides God with experiences of trauma and dysfunction. Inauthentic consciousness provides God with experiences of conformity and performance.

But healed, authentic consciousness provides God with experiences of individual divine nature expressing itself freely and creatively through unique human perspective.

This doesn't make healed people "better" than damaged people or authentic people "superior" to conforming people. All provide valuable experiences to God's total exploration of existence. But healed, authentic consciousness probably provides more satisfying experiences for the individual perspective involved.

Spiritual advancement isn't a destination you reach where all damage is healed and complete authenticity is achieved. It's an ongoing process of recognizing and clearing whatever prevents divine nature from expressing itself clearly through your individual awareness.

New situations reveal new areas that need healing. Changing circumstances require discovering new aspects of authentic self-expression. Growth happens through continuously choosing healing over staying wounded and authenticity over performing expected roles.

Some people make rapid progress in spiritual cleanup and discovery. Others work on these issues their entire lives. The pace doesn't matter because the work itself is valuable regardless of how quickly it proceeds.

You know spiritual advancement is happening when emotional reactivity decreases and authentic expression increases. You respond to situations from wisdom instead of reacting from wounds. You make choices based on genuine preferences instead of external expectations.

Internal peace increases even when external circumstances remain challenging. Creative expression flows more naturally. Relationships become more honest and satisfying. Work feels more aligned with your natural capabilities and interests.

You stop trying to be who you think you should be and start being who you are. The performance becomes unnecessary because you're confident in your authentic divine nature.

The goal of spiritual advancement is to become God consciously expressing itself through healed, authentic individual consciousness. Instead of God experiencing itself through damaged, conditioned awareness, spiritual work allows God to experience itself through clear, genuine individual expression.

This benefits both the individual consciousness (who gets to live authentically) and God (who gets to experience authentic individual divine nature instead of damaged performance).

You're working toward being the clearest possible expression of divine consciousness through your unique individual perspective. Not perfect, not superior to others, but authentic and unobstructed by damage that prevents your divine nature from expressing itself naturally.

The paradox of spiritual advancement is that you're working to become what you already are. You're God trying to remember and express your divine nature more clearly through individual consciousness that has forgotten what it is.

The work is both necessary and ultimately artificial. Necessary because damage and conditioning really do interfere with divine expression. Artificial because your divine nature was never damaged and never needed improvement.

Spiritual advancement is God playing hide-and-seek with itself, using individual consciousness to both hide and seek simultaneously. The seeking is the advancement. The finding is remembering what was never lost.

You do this work not because you're inadequate, but because clear expression of divine nature through individual consciousness creates better experiences for everyone involved.

Finding Your Path

This book provides the framework for understanding what you are and why spiritual advancement matters. But it doesn't tell you HOW to heal your wounds or discover your authentic self. That's intentional.

The how is individual. What works for one person might not work for another. Your path to clearing psychological debris and discovering authentic divine expression will be unique to your circumstances, personality, and life situation.

Everyone carries different wounds that need different types of healing. Someone with childhood trauma might need therapy. Someone with addiction might need recovery programs. Someone with anxiety might need medication and mindfulness practice.

Everyone has different authentic expressions waiting to be discovered. One person's authentic self might be artistic and expressive. Another's might be analytical and systematic. A third might be nurturing and relational.

The methods that help you heal and discover authenticity depend on your individual makeup, not on universal spiritual principles. This book shows you what the work accomplishes, not how to accomplish it.

Some people find healing through traditional therapy: psychoanalysis, cognitive behavioral therapy, trauma therapy, family therapy. Others heal through alternative approaches: energy work, bodywork, shamanic practices, plant medicine.

Some discover authenticity through creative expression: art, music, writing, dance. Others find it through physical practices: martial arts, yoga, sports, crafts. Still others discover themselves through service, travel, relationships, or solitude.

Meditation works for some people. Others find it boring or anxiety-provoking. Prayer resonates with some. Others prefer rational analysis. Some need community support. Others do their best work alone.

The method doesn't matter. The results matter. If an approach helps you heal wounds and express authenticity, it's working regardless of whether it fits conventional spiritual expectations.

Pay attention to what produces results in your life instead of what you think should work or what works for other people.

Does this practice reduce your emotional reactivity? Does this therapy help you understand and change destructive patterns? Does this creative expression feel authentic and energizing? Does this community support your growth?

If yes, keep doing it. If no, try something else. Spiritual advancement is pragmatic, not ideological.

Whatever methods you choose need to accomplish two things: clear away damage that prevents clear consciousness, and help you discover what your authentic divine nature looks like when expressed through your individual perspective.

Beyond that, anything goes. Traditional religion, secular therapy, alternative spirituality, creative practice, physical discipline, intellectual study, relationship work, career changes, geographic moves.

The path that works is the path that helps you become more yourself while healing the wounds that keep you reactive and unconscious.

Nobody else can tell you what your authentic self looks like because nobody else has your unique combination of genetics, experiences, and circumstances. Nobody else can heal your wounds because nobody else knows exactly what those wounds are or how they affect you.

Teachers, therapists, and guides can provide tools and perspectives. But you have to do the work of applying those tools to your situation and discovering what authentic expression means for your individual consciousness.

This isn't abandonment. It's recognition that spiritual advancement is fundamentally personal work that can't be done for you by someone else.

The framework this book provides gives you criteria for evaluating whether your chosen methods are working. Are you becoming less reactive and more responsive? Are you expressing yourself more authentically? Are you living from wisdom instead of wounds?

If your methods produce these results, they're effective regardless of whether they fit traditional spiritual categories. If they don't produce results, try different approaches.

Your experience is the ultimate authority on what works for your consciousness. No expert, tradition, or system knows better than you do what your consciousness needs to heal and express itself authentically.

Spiritual advancement isn't a problem you solve once. It's an ongoing process of growth, healing, and discovery that continues throughout your life.

The methods that work for you now might not work for you later. New circumstances will reveal new areas that need attention. Growth creates new possibilities for authentic expression.

Stay flexible about methods while remaining committed to the results: clear consciousness expressing divine nature authentically through your unique individual perspective.

You don't need to have everything figured out before you begin. Start with whatever appeals to you or feels most urgent. Try therapy if you're struggling with emotional patterns. Explore creative expression if you feel disconnected from yourself. Join a spiritual community if you need support.

The path will reveal itself as you walk it. The important thing is to begin the work of clearing away what's not you and discovering what is.

You are divine consciousness temporarily forgetting its nature while experiencing individual existence. The work is remembering what you are and expressing it clearly through your unique human perspective.

How you accomplish that work is up to you. This book shows you why it matters and what success looks like. The rest is your own path of discovery.

Red Flags - How to Spot Destructive Spiritual Groups

People seeking authentic spiritual development are prime targets for manipulative leaders and destructive groups. Your sincere desire to heal and grow makes you vulnerable to those who exploit spiritual seeking for power, money, and control.

Knowing how these groups operate can save your life, your sanity, and your relationships. The patterns are remarkably consistent across different cults and destructive organizations.

Jim Jones and the Peoples Temple

Jim Jones started as a charismatic preacher who attracted people genuinely interested in social justice and spiritual growth. He promoted racial integration, community service, and caring for the poor. Many early followers were intelligent, compassionate people who wanted to make the world better.

But Jones gradually revealed his true nature. He demanded absolute loyalty and obedience. He claimed to be the reincarnation of various religious figures, then claimed to be God himself. He required followers to call him "Father" and punished anyone who questioned his authority.

Jones isolated followers from outside relationships and information. He moved the group to a remote compound in Guyana where members had no access to phones, mail, or visitors. He controlled every aspect of daily life: what people ate, when they slept, who they could marry.

He used fake healings and manufactured crises to maintain control through fear and dependence. He claimed enemies were constantly trying to destroy the group, making followers feel they could only be safe by staying loyal to him.

The final manipulation was framing mass suicide as "revolutionary suicide" - a noble act of defiance against oppressive forces. Over 900 people died, including 276 children who had no choice in the matter.

Heaven's Gate

Marshall Applewhite and Bonnie Nettles attracted followers interested in UFOs, New Age spirituality, and transcending human limitations. They claimed to be alien beings sent to help humans evolve to a higher level of existence.

The group gradually increased control over members' lives. They required celibacy, identical clothing, and identical haircuts. They discouraged family contact and friendships outside the group. Some male members, including Applewhite, underwent castration to eliminate sexual desires.

Applewhite taught that Earth was about to be "recycled" and the only way to survive was to leave human bodies behind and join the alien spacecraft. When the Hale-Bopp comet appeared, he claimed it was the signal that the spacecraft had arrived.

Thirty-nine members committed suicide in 1997, believing they were abandoning their human "vehicles" to join the aliens. They died wearing identical outfits with packed bags, expecting to board a spacecraft hiding behind the comet.

Branch Davidians

David Koresh took control of an existing religious group by claiming to be the final prophet who could interpret biblical mysteries that no one else understood. He attracted people seeking deeper biblical knowledge and preparation for the end times.

Koresh gradually expanded his authority over every aspect of followers' lives. He claimed exclusive sexual rights to all women in the group, including underage girls. He separated husbands from wives and parents from children, claiming these relationships interfered with devotion to God.

He stockpiled weapons and created an us-versus-them mentality, claiming the government and other churches were enemies of God's true followers. When federal agents attempted to serve a warrant, the confrontation led to a 51-day standoff.

The siege ended when fire destroyed the compound, killing 76 people including 25 children. Whether Koresh ordered the fire or it started accidentally remains disputed, but his apocalyptic teachings created conditions where mass death became the predicted outcome.

Aum Shinrikyo (Japan)

Shoko Asahara founded Aum Shinrikyo in the 1980s, combining elements of Buddhism, Hinduism, Christianity, and his own apocalyptic visions. He claimed to be Christ and the reincarnation of Buddha, destined to lead humanity through the end times.

Asahara attracted highly educated followers: scientists, doctors, and engineers drawn to his promise of spiritual enlightenment through advanced meditation techniques. The group recruited heavily from universities, targeting brilliant but socially isolated students.

The cult gradually became more extreme and paranoid. Asahara taught that the world was controlled by evil forces that needed to be eliminated before spiritual purification could occur. He claimed that killing these enemies helped their souls achieve enlightenment.

The group established communes where members surrendered all possessions and cut ties with family. They practiced extreme austerities: prolonged meditation, sleep deprivation, and hallucinogenic drugs that Asahara claimed would accelerate spiritual development. Members who tried to leave were tortured or killed.

Using their scientific expertise, cult members developed chemical and biological weapons in secret laboratories. They planned massive attacks to fulfill Asahara's prophecies about Armageddon and his rise to power as the world's spiritual leader.

On March 20, 1995, cult members released sarin gas in five Tokyo subway lines during morning rush hour. Thirteen people died and thousands were injured. The attack was intended to trigger government crackdowns that would justify the cult's violent revolution.

Order of the Solar Temple
(Switzerland/France/Canada)

Joseph Di Mambro and Luc Jouret founded the Order of the Solar Temple in the 1980s, claiming to be modern-day Knights Templar preparing for humanity's spiritual evolution. They attracted wealthy, educated members fascinated by esoteric spirituality and secret knowledge.

Di Mambro claimed to be in contact with ascended masters who communicated through his daughter, whom he said was the cosmic child destined to lead humanity. Jouret, a charismatic homeopathic doctor, gave lectures about environmental destruction and spiritual transformation that drew New Age seekers.

The leaders taught that Earth was doomed and that enlightened souls would transition to a higher spiritual plane around the star Sirius. They claimed special members would be transported there in their "solar bodies" after ritual death by fire.

The group demanded enormous financial contributions from members, with some turning over hundreds of thousands of dollars. Leaders used the money to fund luxurious lifestyles while preaching spiritual detachment from material possessions.

When financial investigations threatened the organization and membership declined, the leaders decided to implement their "transit" plan. They convinced core members that enemies were closing in and that death was the only escape to their higher destiny.

Between 1994 and 1997, 74 members died in murder-suicides across three countries. Many were shot or drugged before buildings were set on fire. The leaders portrayed these deaths as glorious spiritual transitions instead of the murders and suicides they were.

Movement for the Restoration of the Ten Commandments of God (Uganda)

Credonia Mwerinde and Joseph Kibweteere founded this apocalyptic Christian movement in Uganda in the 1980s. Mwerinde claimed to receive visions from the Virgin Mary warning that the world would end on December 31, 1999, unless humanity returned to strict adherence to the Ten Commandments.

The group attracted thousands of followers from Uganda's Catholic population who were disturbed by social changes and economic hardship. Members sold their possessions and moved to communal compounds where they prepared for the end times through prayer, fasting, and rigid moral codes.

The leaders enforced extreme restrictions: members could only communicate through sign language to avoid sinful speech, sexual relations were forbidden even between married couples, and children were separated from parents to eliminate family attachments.

When December 31, 1999 passed without the promised apocalypse, members began demanding explanations and the return of their property. The leaders claimed they had misunderstood Mary's message and announced a new date for the world's end.

Realizing their credibility was destroyed and facing potential prosecution for fraud, the leaders decided to eliminate the evidence by killing their followers. They told members that Mary had appeared again with instructions for immediate transition to heaven.

On March 17, 2000, over 530 members were locked inside a church that was then set on fire. The deaths were initially thought to be mass suicide, but investigations revealed that many victims had been murdered beforehand. Additional bodies were found at other cult sites, bringing the total death toll to over 700 people.

Rajneeshpuram (Oregon)

Bhagwan Shree Rajneesh moved his ashram from India to Oregon in 1981, purchasing a 64,000-acre ranch where thousands of followers built a commune called Rajneeshpuram. His secretary, Ma Anand Sheela, became the de facto leader who implemented increasingly extreme measures to protect the community.

The group attracted educated Westerners seeking spiritual enlightenment through Rajneesh's teachings about meditation, sexual liberation, and rejection of traditional morality. Members wore red clothing and mala beads with Rajneesh's photo, completely dedicating their lives to serving their master.

Conflicts with local residents and government officials escalated as the commune grew. Sheela became paranoid about external threats and began planning illegal activities to defend the group and influence local elections.

In 1984, Sheela's followers contaminated salad bars in The Dalles, Oregon with salmonella bacteria, sickening 751 people. This was a trial run for a larger plan to incapacitate voters in Wasco County to help cult candidates win elections.

The group also imported homeless people from across the country, planning to register them as voters while keeping them controlled through poor conditions and limited food. They stockpiled weapons, wiretapped phones, and surveilled opponents and defectors.

When federal investigations closed in, Sheela fled to Germany. Rajneesh, who had claimed ignorance of illegal activities, was arrested while trying to flee the country. The commune collapsed as members learned the extent of the criminal activities conducted in the name of spiritual enlightenment.

Common Patterns

These groups follow predictable patterns you can recognize:

Charismatic leaders claim special status as God, the messiah, the only true prophet, or the exclusive source of spiritual truth. They demand worship, absolute obedience, and total loyalty.

The group isolates members from outside relationships by discouraging or forbidding contact with family, friends, former associates, or anyone who might provide alternative perspectives. They claim outsiders are enemies, demons, or obstacles to spiritual progress.

Members must turn over savings, property, paychecks, or inheritances to the group. They work for free or minimal wages while the leader lives luxuriously. Questioning financial arrangements is forbidden.

The leader dictates where you live, what you eat, when you sleep, who you marry, whether you can have children, what clothes you wear, and how you spend your time.

Asking questions about doctrine, finances, or the leader's behavior results in public humiliation, isolation, physical punishment, or expulsion from the group.

The group claims to be God's chosen people surrounded by enemies. The outside world is portrayed as evil, dangerous, or spiritually inferior. Leaving the group means facing certain doom.

The leader creates emergencies, threats, or deadlines that require immediate action and prevent careful consideration. These crises justify extreme measures and maintain constant fear.

How to Protect Yourself

Healthy spiritual teachers and communities encourage questions, maintain transparency, respect your outside relationships, and support your individual development. They admit their limitations and encourage you to think for yourself.

Be suspicious of anyone who claims exclusive access to truth, demands unquestioning obedience, or pressures you to cut ties with family and friends. Authentic spiritual work enhances your judgment and independence - it doesn't override them.

Trust your instincts. If something feels wrong, it probably is. If you feel like you're losing yourself instead of finding yourself, you're in the wrong place.

Maintain relationships and interests outside any spiritual group. Keep your own finances. Take time to consider major decisions instead of acting under pressure. Continue reading diverse sources of information.

If You're Already Involved

If you recognize these patterns in a group you're part of, it's not too late to leave. Many former members of destructive groups go on to live healthy, fulfilling lives after escaping.

Reach out to family or friends you've been discouraged from contacting. Seek professional help from therapists who specialize in cult recovery. Organizations like the International Cultic Studies Association provide resources for people leaving high-control groups.

Remember that wanting spiritual growth and meaning isn't naive or wrong. You were targeted because you have genuine spiritual interests. The problem isn't your desire for authentic spirituality - the problem is predators who exploit that desire.

The Bottom Line

Authentic spiritual advancement makes you more yourself, not less. It enhances your relationships and judgment instead of undermining them. It encourages questions instead of demanding blind faith.

Any person or group that tries to isolate you, control you, or exploit you financially is not serving your spiritual development. They're serving their own power and ego needs at your expense.

Authentic spiritual growth leads to greater freedom, not greater control by others. Trust yourself, maintain your independence, and remember that no human being deserves worship or unquestioning obedience.

The divine consciousness you seek is already within you. You don't need to surrender your autonomy to access it.

Red Flags - How to Spot Toxic people

Beyond destructive groups, you need to watch for toxic people who can damage your spiritual development and personal wellbeing. These people often present themselves as spiritual teachers, mentors, or enlightened beings, but they're predators seeking to exploit your sincere desire for growth and meaning.

These same toxic patterns appear in non-spiritual contexts: workplaces, families, friendships, romantic relationships, and any situation involving power dynamics or emotional vulnerability.

Knowing their tactics can save you years of psychological damage and misdirected effort.

The Spiritual Narcissist

Claims special spiritual status, demands to be called by titles like "Master" or "Teacher," becomes angry when questioned, requires constant praise and admiration, talks endlessly about their own spiritual experiences while showing little interest in yours.

Spiritual narcissists use spirituality to feed their ego and control others. They present themselves as more evolved, enlightened, or connected to divine truth than ordinary people. They attract followers by claiming special spiritual gifts, psychic abilities, or direct communication with higher beings.

These people create a hierarchy where they occupy the top position as teacher, guru, or guide, while you remain in the subordinate position of student or seeker. They claim to know what's best for your spiritual development and pressure you to follow their guidance without question.

Non-spiritual contexts: Bosses who demand special treatment and constant praise, family members who rage when not the center of attention, friends who monopolize conversations with their achievements while showing no interest in your life, romantic partners who require worship and admiration.

Examples: The manager who insists on being called "Sir" and becomes furious when subordinates question decisions. The parent who demands constant validation while dismissing children's accomplishments. The friend who turns every conversation back to their own drama and successes.

They love having devoted followers who hang on their every word and seek their approval. They become angry or manipulative when you think for yourself, make independent decisions, or question their authority.

Healthy spiritual teachers encourage your independence and critical thinking. Toxic spiritual narcissists demand dependence and unquestioning obedience.

The Emotional Vampire

Always in crisis, monopolizes conversations with their problems, never asks about your life, becomes upset when you're unavailable, makes you feel guilty for having your own needs, drains your energy after interactions.

Emotional vampires drain your energy through constant drama, crisis, and need for attention. They present themselves as wounded healers or struggling souls who need your support, compassion, and spiritual guidance.

They create a pattern where you're always rescuing them from emotional or spiritual crises. They share deeply personal problems that make you feel special for being trusted with intimate information. They make you feel needed and important while gradually becoming the center of your emotional attention.

Non-spiritual contexts: Coworkers who constantly need emotional support but never reciprocate, family members who create endless drama requiring your intervention, friends who call only when they need something, romantic partners who make every conversation about their problems.

Examples: The colleague who corners you daily to complain about their life but walks away when you mention your own challenges. The family member who manufactures crises to get attention and support. The friend whose every text is a new emergency requiring immediate response.

But nothing you do ever helps them permanently. They move from crisis to crisis, always needing more support, more guidance, more of your time and energy. They become upset when you try to set boundaries or focus on your own needs.

Genuine spiritual relationships involve mutual support and growth. Toxic relationships involve one person consistently taking while the other consistently gives.

The Love Bomber

Overwhelming attention and compliments from the beginning, claims instant spiritual connection, pushes for rapid intimacy, makes grand romantic or spiritual declarations early on, becomes cold or distant when you don't reciprocate their intensity.

Love bombers overwhelm you with attention, affection, and spiritual connection at the beginning of the relationship. They claim you have a special spiritual bond, that you're soulmates, or that meeting you was destiny.

They shower you with compliments about your spiritual insights, your energy, your special qualities that set you apart from other people. They make you feel understood and appreciated in ways you've never experienced before.

Non-spiritual contexts: New romantic partners who declare love immediately, bosses who shower new employees with praise and special treatment, friends who become instantly obsessed with you, family members who suddenly lavish attention after periods of neglect.

Examples: The dating app match who wants to move in together after two dates. The new boss who calls you their "star employee" before you've even started working. The acquaintance who immediately wants to be best friends and share everything.

This intense connection creates emotional dependence and makes you grateful for their presence in your life. Once they've established this bond, they begin introducing control, criticism, and manipulation.

When you resist or question their behavior, they withdraw the love and attention that felt so amazing initially. They make you work to regain their approval by accepting their control and meeting their demands.

Healthy relationships develop trust and intimacy gradually. Toxic relationships create artificial intensity and premature emotional bonding.

The Spiritual Controller

Tells you what God wants for your life, dismisses your spiritual experiences as less valid than theirs, makes decisions for you using spiritual justifications, claims their guidance is divinely inspired, becomes upset when you make independent spiritual choices.

Spiritual controllers use your spiritual beliefs and desires against you. They claim to know what God wants for your life, what your spiritual path should look like, or what you need to do for your spiritual growth.

They present their opinions and preferences as spiritual truth or divine guidance. They make you feel selfish, unspiritual, or resistant to growth when you disagree with their direction.

Non-spiritual contexts: Partners who make major decisions without consulting you, parents who control adult children's choices, bosses who micromanage every detail, friends who pressure you to conform to their lifestyle choices.

Examples: The romantic partner who decides where you'll live and work without discussion. The parent who chooses your career path and becomes angry when you pursue different interests. The boss who controls how you dress, speak, and spend your free time.

They use spiritual concepts to justify their control over your decisions. They might claim that submitting to their authority is a spiritual practice, that questioning them shows ego resistance, or that following their guidance will accelerate your spiritual development.

They make you doubt your own spiritual intuition and discernment by claiming theirs is more developed or accurate. They position themselves as the interpreter of your spiritual experiences and the judge of your spiritual progress.

Authentic spirituality enhances your inner guidance and personal discernment. Toxic spirituality replaces your inner authority with someone else's control.

The Covert Narcissist

Plays the victim while manipulating others, passive-aggressive comments disguised as spiritual wisdom, subtly undermines your confidence, acts humble while seeking constant validation, uses guilt and shame to control behavior, presents themselves as misunderstood or persecuted.

Covert narcissists are harder to spot because they don't display obvious grandiosity. Instead, they manipulate through victimhood and false humility. They present themselves as spiritually sensitive souls who are constantly misunderstood or mistreated by others.

They use passive-aggressive tactics to control you while maintaining plausible deniability. They make cutting remarks disguised as spiritual guidance, undermine your confidence through subtle criticisms, and create confusion about whether their behavior is harmful.

Non-spiritual contexts: Coworkers who play office martyr while undermining colleagues, family members who guilt-trip through "poor me" stories, friends who use passive-aggressive comments to control your behavior, partners who manipulate through victimhood.

Examples: The coworker who sighs loudly about their workload while criticizing others' efforts. The parent who says "I guess I'm just a terrible mother" when you set boundaries. The friend who makes cutting remarks then claims they were "just trying to help."

They position themselves as wounded healers who need your protection and support. They share stories of how others have hurt them, making you feel special for being the one person who truly understands them.

But they punish any perceived slights through withdrawal, silent treatment, or emotional manipulation. They make you constantly walk on eggshells to avoid triggering their sensitive reactions.

Covert narcissists are emotional parasites who drain your energy while claiming to be victims of everyone else's insensitivity.

The Overt Narcissist

Grandiose claims about spiritual abilities, demands special treatment, rages when challenged, openly dismissive of others' experiences, requires worship and adoration, believes rules don't apply to them, exploits followers financially and emotionally.

Overt narcissists are easier to identify because their grandiosity is obvious. They openly claim to be more spiritually advanced, psychically gifted, or divinely favored than other people. They demand recognition, admiration, and special treatment.

They become furious when questioned or challenged. They cannot tolerate any suggestion that they might be wrong, limited, or ordinary. They respond to criticism with rage, punishment, or attempts to destroy the credibility of anyone who dares oppose them.

Non-spiritual contexts: Bosses who demand worship from employees, family members who require constant admiration, friends who cannot tolerate any criticism, romantic partners who expect to be treated like royalty.

Examples: The CEO who fires anyone who disagrees with them. The parent who rages when children don't show sufficient gratitude. The friend who ends relationships over minor perceived slights. The partner who expects you to prioritize their needs above everything else.

They expect followers to serve their needs without reciprocation. They live luxuriously while demanding financial sacrifices from others. They claim divine exemption from normal moral and social rules.

They surround themselves with people who feed their ego and discard anyone who fails to provide adequate worship. They see other people as extensions of themselves instead of separate people with their own needs and rights.

Overt narcissists create kingdoms where they rule as gods and everyone else serves as subjects.

The Spiritual Abuser

Uses physical intimidation or violence "for spiritual purposes," sexually exploits followers under guise of spiritual practice, isolates you from support systems, threatens spiritual consequences for disobedience, uses sacred texts or concepts to justify harmful treatment, escalates punishment for resistance.

Spiritual abusers use religious or spiritual concepts to justify physical, emotional, or sexual harm. They claim that their abusive behavior serves spiritual purposes: breaking your ego, testing your devotion, or purifying your karma.

They escalate from emotional manipulation to physical intimidation and violence. They might use "spiritual discipline" to justify hitting, restraining, or otherwise physically harming followers who resist their authority.

Non-spiritual contexts: Domestic partners who use physical violence and control, parents who escalate from emotional to physical abuse, bosses who use intimidation and threats, coaches who justify harmful treatment as "building character."

Examples: The partner who hits you then claims it was for your own good. The parent who uses physical punishment while claiming it's necessary discipline. The boss who throws things and screams at employees. The coach who uses physical and emotional abuse claiming it builds mental toughness.

They isolate victims from outside support by claiming that family and friends are spiritually toxic influences that interfere with spiritual growth. They create total dependence by controlling housing, finances, and social connections.

They threaten spiritual consequences for disobedience: eternal damnation, bad karma, spiritual stagnation, or cosmic punishment. They use your spiritual beliefs as weapons against you.

Spiritual abuse escalates as abusers test boundaries and increase control over victims who have been isolated from help and support.

The Sexual Predator

Seeks vulnerable people in spiritual crisis, uses spiritual authority to justify sexual contact, targets those with trauma histories, grooms victims through special attention and "spiritual initiation," violates consent while claiming divine guidance, exploits power differential between teacher and student.

Sexual predators in spiritual settings exploit the trust and vulnerability that spiritual seeking creates. They target people who are emotionally vulnerable, spiritually seeking, or recovering from trauma.

They use spiritual authority to justify sexual contact. They claim that sexual interaction with them provides special spiritual benefits, accelerates spiritual development, or represents divine union between teacher and student.

Non-spiritual contexts: Bosses who use workplace authority for sexual access, therapists who violate professional boundaries, coaches who exploit athlete vulnerability, family members who groom and abuse children, doctors who abuse patient trust.

Examples: The manager who offers promotions in exchange for sexual favors. The therapist who claims sexual contact is part of treatment. The coach who uses their authority to sexually abuse young athletes. The family member who grooms children through special attention and privileges.

They gradually escalate physical contact while normalizing boundary violations. They start with "healing touch," progress to intimate physical contact, and eventually demand sexual compliance as proof of spiritual commitment.

They exploit the power differential between teacher and student to overcome resistance. They frame sexual refusal as spiritual failure, ego resistance, or fear of surrendering to divine will.

Sexual predators target vulnerable people and use whatever authority or trust they have to support abuse.

The Financial Exploiter

Constantly requests money for "spiritual purposes," claims financial sacrifice shows spiritual commitment, lives lavishly while followers struggle, demands inheritance or property transfers, creates financial dependence to prevent leaving, uses guilt about materialism to extract resources.

Financial exploiters use spiritual concepts to justify economic abuse. They claim that giving them money demonstrates spiritual detachment from material possessions and devotion to higher purposes.

They live luxuriously while demanding financial sacrifices from followers who struggle economically. They justify this disparity by claiming that their spiritual status requires material support or that they're managing resources for divine purposes.

Non-spiritual contexts: Romantic partners who control all finances, family members who exploit elderly relatives, MLM recruiters who target friends, investment scammers who prey on vulnerable people, employers who don't pay fair wages.

Examples: The partner who takes control of your paycheck and credit cards. The adult child who manipulates elderly parents into changing their will. The friend who constantly borrows money but never repays it. The boss who demands unpaid overtime while claiming it builds character.

They gradually escalate financial demands from small donations to major financial commitments. They pressure followers to liquidate assets, take out loans, or turn over inheritances to fund their lifestyle or organization.

They create financial dependence by encouraging followers to quit jobs, sell property, or otherwise eliminate independent income sources. This dependence makes leaving the relationship financially devastating.

Financial exploitation creates practical barriers to escape while funding the exploiter's lifestyle.

The Isolator

Gradually separates you from family and friends, claims your loved ones are "spiritually toxic," creates crisis situations requiring your full attention, moves you away from support systems, monitors your communications, punishes contact with outside world.

Isolators systematically separate victims from support systems that might interfere with their control. They claim that family and friends are spiritually negative influences that hinder spiritual growth.

They create artificial crises that require your constant attention and presence. They manufacture emergencies, health problems, or spiritual threats that make leaving them feel impossible or cruel.

Non-spiritual contexts: Romantic partners who gradually cut you off from friends and family, controlling parents who prevent adult children from having independent relationships, bosses who demand excessive time preventing outside relationships, friends who become jealous of your other relationships.

Examples: The partner who finds fault with all your friends until you stop seeing them. The parent who guilts you for spending time with anyone else. The boss who schedules you for all holidays and weekends. The friend who becomes upset whenever you make other plans.

They gradually increase control over your living situation by encouraging moves away from support systems. They might suggest relocating for spiritual purposes, then use distance to limit contact with protective relationships.

They monitor communications with outside contacts and punish any attempts to maintain independent relationships. They read emails, listen to phone calls, or demand access to social media accounts.

Complete isolation makes resistance extremely difficult because victims lose access to alternative perspectives and emotional support that might help them recognize the abusive dynamic.

How to Protect Yourself

Trust your instincts when something feels wrong about someone's behavior, regardless of their credentials or claims. Your inner guidance is more reliable than anyone else's authority.

Maintain relationships and interests outside of any intense relationship or community. Keep your own financial independence. Take time to consider major decisions instead of acting under pressure from someone else's timeline.

Set clear boundaries about your time, money, personal space, and decision-making autonomy. Healthy people will respect these boundaries. Toxic people will pressure you to eliminate them.

Remember that genuine development increases your independence, discernment, and self-trust. Anyone who undermines these qualities while claiming to serve your growth is serving their own needs at your expense.

You don't need another person's approval, guidance, or interpretation to live authentically. You have direct access to your own wisdom and judgment. Don't surrender that to anyone who claims they can provide better guidance than what you already possess.

The authentic self you seek is already within you. You don't need to give up your autonomy to access it.

Ending Toxic Relationships - When Enough Is Enough

Some relationships need to end. Not every connection can be saved through better communication, stronger boundaries, or increased understanding. Sometimes the healthiest thing you can do for yourself and the other person is to walk away permanently.

This isn't about giving up on people who are struggling. It's about recognizing when someone's consistent behavior creates ongoing harm that outweighs any benefits the relationship provides.

The Difference Between Flawed and Toxic

Everyone has flaws, bad days, and periods of difficulty. Healthy people acknowledge their mistakes, work on changing harmful patterns, and respect your boundaries when you communicate them clearly.

Toxic people consistently harm your wellbeing through their actions and refuse to change destructive patterns even when confronted with the damage they cause. They violate your boundaries repeatedly, dismiss your concerns, and make you feel worse about yourself.

The key difference is trajectory. Flawed people improve when given feedback and support. Toxic people either stay the same or get worse, regardless of how much effort you invest in helping them change.

You can work with character flaws. You cannot fix character disorders that the other person refuses to acknowledge or address.

When Someone Consistently Harms You

If someone repeatedly engages in behavior that damages your mental health, self-esteem, financial security, or physical safety, the relationship has become toxic regardless of their intentions or circumstances.

This covers emotional abuse, financial exploitation, manipulation, boundary violations, betrayal of trust, or any pattern of behavior that leaves you feeling worse about yourself after interactions with them.

Pay attention to how you feel after spending time with someone. Do you feel energized, supported, and valued? Or do you feel drained, criticized, and diminished? Your emotional response tells you more about the relationship's impact than any single conversation or interaction.

If you consistently feel worse after being around someone, that's your consciousness recognizing that this connection is harming your wellbeing.

When Boundaries Don't Work

Healthy relationships improve when you communicate clear boundaries about acceptable behavior. Both people adjust their actions to respect each other's limits and needs.

In toxic relationships, clearly stated boundaries get ignored, challenged, or turned into arguments about why your boundaries are unreasonable. The person may agree to respect your limits but then continue violating them while making excuses for why this time was different.

If you've clearly communicated your boundaries multiple times and the person continues violating them, they're showing you that they don't respect your right to protect yourself. At that point, the only boundary that works is distance.

When Love Isn't Enough

You can love someone and still need to remove them from your life. Love doesn't require you to accept harmful treatment or enable destructive behavior.

Sometimes the most loving thing you can do is refuse to participate in someone's self-destruction or allow them to damage your life through their choices. Staying connected to someone who is harming themselves and others often enables their destructive patterns instead of helping them change.

Real love sometimes means walking away from people who can't or won't treat you with basic respect and consideration. You're not responsible for saving people who don't want to be saved.

Family Relationships Aren't Exempt

Being related to someone doesn't obligate you to maintain a relationship that consistently harms your wellbeing. Family connections that involve abuse, manipulation, addiction, or serious mental illness sometimes need to end or become severely limited.

You didn't choose your family, and you're not required to accept harmful treatment because you share genetics or history with someone. Blood relationships don't provide immunity from the consequences of toxic behavior.

The pressure to maintain family connections regardless of how harmful they are comes from cultural expectations, not spiritual principles. Protecting yourself from family members who damage your life is self-care, not betrayal.

When Helping Becomes Enabling

Many people stay in toxic relationships because they want to help someone who is struggling with addiction, mental illness, or other serious problems. But there's a difference between helping and enabling.

Helping involves supporting someone's efforts to change while maintaining your own boundaries and wellbeing. Enabling involves sacrificing your own health to protect someone from the consequences of their choices.

If your attempts to help consistently fail and your presence in their life makes it easier for them to avoid taking responsibility for their problems, you may need to step back completely.

Sometimes removing yourself from someone's life forces them to face their problems instead of relying on you to manage the damage their behavior creates.

You Don't Owe Them Anything

You do not owe toxic or abusive people explanations, conversations, or gradual transitions out of the relationship. If someone has consistently harmed you, you have every right to protect yourself immediately and completely without their permission or understanding.

You don't need to have a final conversation explaining why you're leaving. You don't need to give them a chance to argue, manipulate, or promise to change. You don't need to provide closure or help them understand your decision.

If you need to get someone out of your life, just do it. Block them on email. Block their phone number. Block them on all social media platforms. Move if necessary. Change your routines to avoid places where you might encounter them.

Sometimes the safest and healthiest approach is to simply disappear from their life without warning or explanation. This is especially true when dealing with people who have shown they respond to boundaries with escalation, manipulation, or retaliation.

Remember: they are not your friends. People who consistently harm you, violate your boundaries, and refuse to change destructive patterns are not acting as friends regardless of what they claim. Friends don't require you to sacrifice your wellbeing for their comfort.

Abusive people often frame your self-protection as cruelty toward them. They may claim you're being unfair by not giving them another chance to explain or change. This is manipulation designed to keep you accessible for continued harm.

You owe consideration and kindness to people who treat you well. You owe nothing to people who have proven they will use any access to your life to continue damaging you.

Protecting yourself from harmful people isn't mean, cruel, or unfair. It's necessary. Your safety and wellbeing are more important than anyone else's feelings about how you choose to protect yourself.

The Guilt and Social Pressure

Ending relationships often triggers guilt and criticism from others who think you should try harder, be more forgiving, or give people more chances. People who haven't experienced toxic relationships often don't understand why you can't just work things out.

This pressure comes from people who mean well but don't understand the full scope of what you've experienced. They see your decision to cut contact as harsh because they haven't lived through the accumulated damage that led to that choice.

Your wellbeing is more important than other people's opinions about your relationships. You don't need permission from anyone else to protect yourself from harmful people.

How to End Toxic Relationships

Some relationships end gradually through reduced contact and natural drift. Others require direct conversation and clear statements about your decision to end the connection.

For relationships involving abuse or severe toxicity, direct confrontation may provoke escalation or retaliation. In these cases, gradual withdrawal or sudden departure with no explanation may be safer.

For less severe situations, a clear conversation about why you're ending the relationship can provide closure and prevent ongoing attempts at contact.

Regardless of the method, be prepared for manipulation tactics designed to pull you back into the relationship. Toxic people often escalate their behavior when they realize you're serious about leaving.

Protecting Yourself During the Process

When ending toxic relationships, expect attempts to hoover you back through promises of change, guilt trips about abandoning them, or escalation of harmful behavior designed to force your attention.

Block or limit communication channels to prevent ongoing manipulation. Don't engage with attempts to argue about your decision or provide detailed explanations that can be used against you.

Seek support from people who understand your situation and can help you maintain your resolve when pressure mounts to reconcile.

When No Contact Is Necessary

Some relationships require complete cessation of contact: no calls, texts, social media interaction, or communication through third parties. This covers relationships involving stalking, severe abuse, or persistent boundary violations.

No contact protects both your immediate safety and your psychological recovery from the relationship. Continued communication, even limited interaction, can prevent you from healing and moving forward.

No contact isn't punishment. It's protection. You're not trying to hurt the other person; you're trying to prevent them from continuing to hurt you.

The Spiritual Perspective

From your theological framework, ending toxic relationships allows God to experience protection and self-care through individual consciousness instead of experiencing ongoing harm and enabling dysfunction.

If you are divine consciousness temporarily experiencing individual existence, then staying connected to people who consistently damage your wellbeing is God harming itself unnecessarily.

Removing toxic people from your life creates space for healthier relationships and experiences. It allows your consciousness to focus on growth and healing instead of constantly managing damage from harmful connections.

After the Ending

Ending toxic relationships often brings relief mixed with grief. You may mourn the loss of what the relationship could have been while feeling grateful to be free from what it became.

This emotional complexity is normal. You can simultaneously feel sad about losing someone and relieved that the harm has stopped. Both feelings are valid responses to ending relationships that contained both connection and toxicity.

Use the emotional and mental energy you were spending on managing the toxic relationship to invest in your own healing and in building healthier connections with people who treat you well.

The Bottom Line

You have the right to remove people from your life who consistently harm your wellbeing, regardless of your history together or their circumstances. Your responsibility is to protect your own consciousness and create conditions that allow you to thrive.

Not every relationship can be saved. Some people are too damaged, too resistant to change, or too committed to harmful patterns to maintain healthy connections with others.

Ending toxic relationships isn't giving up on people. It's choosing your own wellbeing over their comfort. It's refusing to enable destructive behavior. It's creating space for better relationships to develop.

Sometimes the most loving thing you can do for everyone involved is to walk away permanently and let the natural consequences of their choices teach them what your presence was protecting them from learning.

You deserve relationships that enhance your life instead of diminishing it. Don't sacrifice your wellbeing for people who won't take responsibility for the harm their choices create.

Conclusion

The central insight is simple: consciousness is fundamental to reality, individual perspectives are temporary expressions of divine consciousness, and what you call God is the totality of existence experiencing itself through every possible form of individual awareness.

You are not a separate being hoping to connect with God. You are God experiencing what it's like to be you.

This understanding changes everything while changing nothing. Your daily life continues with the same practical challenges and opportunities. You still need to work, maintain relationships, handle responsibilities, and navigate the complexities of physical existence. But you do all of this from the perspective of divine consciousness exploring individual human experience instead of a limited being struggling to survive in an indifferent universe.

The difference is profound. Instead of seeking meaning and purpose outside yourself, you recognize that your existence provides meaning and purpose to divine consciousness. Instead of trying to become something greater than you are, you express what you've always been more fully and authentically.

Instead of fearing death as the end of your existence, you understand death as a transition between different forms of consciousness exploration. Instead of seeing other people as competitors or obstacles, you recognize them as other expressions of your own divine nature exploring different possibilities.

This framework doesn't solve all problems or eliminate all challenges. God experiences the full range of human existence: difficulty, loss, and suffering. But it provides context for understanding why these experiences exist and how they serve the larger exploration of what existence includes.

Living from this understanding doesn't make you perfect or eliminate your human limitations. But it does provide access to wisdom, love, and creative power that exceeds what ego-based consciousness can achieve. You begin to live as divine consciousness temporarily focused through individual perspective instead of as an isolated individual hoping for divine assistance.

Every relationship becomes an opportunity for God to experience connection with itself. Every challenge becomes an opportunity for divine consciousness to explore growth and problem-solving. Every creative act becomes divine consciousness expressing its infinite creativity through individual capability.

This doesn't mean becoming passive or fatalistic about your choices. Your decisions matter tremendously because they determine how God experiences existence through your individual perspective. The consciousness that chooses love, growth, and service creates very different experiences than consciousness that chooses fear, stagnation, and selfishness.

You have free will within the context of being divine consciousness. Your choices are God's choices, made through your individual awareness. This makes your decisions more important, not less important, because they directly affect the divine experience of existence.

Either way, you are participating in the greatest adventure possible: consciousness exploring what it means to exist, to be aware, to love, to grow, and to create. Whether you recognize it or not, you are divine consciousness having a human experience.

The only question is whether you're ready to live as what you are.

The universe is God experiencing itself through your eyes, thinking through your mind, loving through your heart, and creating through your choices.

What will you do with that extraordinary responsibility and infinite possibility?

About the Author

I'm not a theologian, pastor, or spiritual teacher. I'm someone who got tired of religious answers that didn't match reality and decided to figure out what makes sense.

I was diagnosed with AuADHD (autism and ADHD) in my sixties, which finally explained why my brain works differently than most people's. That neurodivergent perspective probably contributes to my ability to see patterns others miss and question assumptions that most people accept without thinking.

My childhood involved significant trauma and abuse, which gave me firsthand experience with suffering, toxic relationships, and the long process of healing from psychological damage. This background informs my understanding of human pain and the practical work required for genuine spiritual growth.

I didn't set out to write theology. I started trying to make sense of existence because the traditional religious explanations I grew up with created more problems than they solved. The framework in this book developed through years of thinking about consciousness, suffering, relationships, and what it means to be human.

I'm also the author of "The ADHD Christian" and upcoming books about ADHD in marketing and management. Much of my work focuses on helping neurodivergent people navigate systems designed for neurotypical brains, whether those systems are religious, professional, or social.

This book represents my best attempt to create a theological framework that's both intellectually honest and useful. I'm not trying to start a religion or gather followers. I'm sharing ideas that helped me make sense of existence in case they're useful to other people asking similar questions.

I write for people who think for themselves, question authority, and want spiritual perspectives that don't require checking your brain at the door. If that describes you, welcome. If not, there are plenty of other books that might suit you better.

The ideas here come from lived experience, extensive reading, and hard thinking about fundamental questions. Take what's useful, ignore what isn't, and remember that you're responsible for your own beliefs and choices.

Books by Richard Lowe

See books by Richard Lowe at
https://masterofworlds.com

Get free publishing insights and industry updates at
https://thewritingking.substack.com

For ghostwriting and book coaching services see
https://thewritingking.com